TEACHING RESOURCES D
Unit Three: Poetry

to accompany

ADVENTURES
in Reading

ATHENA EDITION

HOLT, RINEHART AND WINSTON
Harcourt Brace & Company

Austin • New York • Orlando • Chicago • Atlanta • San Francisco • Boston • Dallas • Toronto • London

Acknowledgments

For permission to reprint copyrighted material, grateful acknowledgment is made to the following sources:

Arte Público Press, University of Houston: From "Bribe" from *Chants* by Pat Mora. Copyright © 1985 by Pat Mora.

Elizabeth Barnett, Literary Executor: From "The Fawn" from *Collected Poems* by Edna St. Vincent Millay. Copyright © 1934, 1962 by Edna St. Vincent Millay and Norma Millay Ellis. Published by HarperCollins.

Carl Cowl, Administrator for the Archives of Claude McKay: From "A Song of the Moon" from *Selected Poems of Claude McKay.* Copyright © 1979 by Harcourt Brace & Company.

Doubleday, a division of Bantam Doubleday Dell Publishing Group, Inc.: From "The Meadow Mouse" from *The Collected Poems of Theodore Roethke.* Copyright © 1963 by Beatrice Roethke, Administratrix of the Estate of Theodore Roethke.

Harcourt Brace & Company: From "Art Review" from *Afternoon of a Pawnbroker and Other Poems* by Kenneth Fearing. Copyright 1943 by Kenneth Fearing; copyright renewed © 1971 by Bruce Fearing.

Henry Holt and Company, Inc.: From "At Woodward's Gardens," from "Desert Places," and from "It Bids Pretty Fair" from *The Poetry of Robert Frost,* edited by Edward Connery Lathem. Copyright 1936 by Robert Frost; copyright renewed © 1964, 1975 by Lesley Frost Ballantine; copyright 1947, © 1968, 1969 by Henry Holt and Company, Inc. From "Loveliest of trees, the cherry now" from "A Shropshire Lad" - Authorised Edition - from *The Collected Poems of A. E. Housman.* Copyright 1939, 1940, © 1965 by Henry Holt and Company, Inc.; copyright © 1967, 1968 by Robert E. Symons.

Alfred A. Knopf, Inc.: From "Dream Deferred" from *The Panther and the Lash* by Langston Hughes. Copyright 1951 by Langston Hughes.

TABLE OF CONTENTS

UNIT THREE: POETRY

OUR HOUSE IN HADONG   *Wendy Wilder Larsen and Tran Thi Nga*

THE MEADOW MOUSE   *Theodore Roethke*

THE FAWN   *Edna St. Vincent Millay*

WITHOUT TITLE   *Diane Glancy* and THE SPACE   *Gary Soto*

THE DAY IS DONE   *Henry Wadsworth Longfellow*

I'LL TELL YOU HOW THE SUN ROSE   *Emily Dickinson*

IT BIDS PRETTY FAIR   *Robert Frost*, MOON TIGER   *Denise Levertov*, and SILVER   *Walter de la Mare*

This booklet, *Teaching Resources D*, contains unit and selection teaching suggestions as well as a wide variety of materials that can be used to enliven instruction, address specific curriculum concerns, attend to individual student needs, and monitor student mastery.

SELECTION TEACHING MATERIALS

Teaching Notes with Answer Keys—Teaching suggestions and useful instructional features are found on the **Teacher's Notes** pages that are provided for almost every individual literary selection. The **Teacher's Notes** for a specific selection may contain a variety of the following features:

- itemized **Objectives** for teaching the selection
- an **Introduction** to the selection, with helpful background details about the author, the literary period, or the literary work
- critical or scholarly **Commentary** about the selection
- a **Reading/Critical Thinking Strategies** feature to lead students into, through, and beyond the meaning of the literary selection
- a list of **Vocabulary** words from the selection that are defined in the glossary in the textbook, along with the textbook page number or the poem line number on which each word is to be found
- a **Vocabulary Activity** to support study of the selection and development of the student's vocabulary skills

In addition to these features, the **Teacher's Notes** pages contain **Answer Keys** to worksheets that are provided to support study of a particular selection.

Copying Masters/Student Worksheets—These worksheets and support materials may include a variety of the following types of copying masters:

- **Reading Check** worksheets—provide comprehensive questions that help confirm student understanding of the meaning of the selection
- **Study Guide** worksheets—contain a series of leading questions that guide students through a close analytical reading of the selection
- **Language Skills** worksheets—contain exercises that often use brief excerpts from the literary selection to integrate grade-level-appropriate language, grammar, usage, and mechanics skills
- **Building Vocabulary** worksheets—offer a range of strategies to help students acquire vocabulary-improvement skills
- **Selection Vocabulary Tests**—provide a check of student mastery of the vocabulary words found in the selection
- **Selection Tests**—help to evaluate student understanding of the literary selection

UNIT TEACHING MATERIALS

Support materials for assessing unit mastery may include the following copying masters:

- **Mastery Tests**—provide for a comprehensive assessment of selections included in a unit or in a specific literary period
- **Analogy Lessons**—give students an opportunity to practice analyzing the kinds of relationships that may be expressed in analogies
- **Analogy Tests**—help students gain proficiency in analyzing and solving analogy problems
- **Composition Tests**—offer a choice of writing prompts that call for the student to give a developed and thoughtful written response

UNIT OBJECTIVES

The aims of this unit are for the student:
- To demonstrate recognition and understanding of the speaker of a poem
- To identify and analyze imagery in poems
- To identify and analyze the use of figurative language such as simile, metaphor, and personification to express relationships
- To demonstrate recognition and understanding of the sound effect of such devices as rhyme, rhythm, alliteration, onomatopoeia, repetition, and parallelism
- To analyze the structure as well as the meaning of the poems
- To identify, analyze, and interpret tone and theme in poems
- To demonstrate recognition and understanding of different forms of lyric, narrative, and dramatic poetry
- To expand vocabulary by analyzing the structures and meanings of words in poems
- To write paragraphs of poetry
- To write compositions of analysis
- To write poems in imitation of some of those in the unit

OVERVIEW OF THE UNIT

The poetry unit contains forty-six poems and is divided into ten sections. Each of the sections focuses on one aspect of poetry: the speaker, diction, imagery, figurative language, sound patterns, structures, tone, and types of poetry (lyric, narrative, and dramatic). The unit concludes with two special features: **Developing Skills in Critical Thinking** provides guidelines for analyzing poems; **Practice in Reading and Writing** offers practice in paraphrasing a poem and in comparing two poems.

A BIRD CAME DOWN THE WALK *Emily Dickinson* Text Page 295

OBJECTIVES The aims of this close-reading lesson are for the student:
- To demonstrate the ability to examine a poem in depth
- To demonstrate the ability to follow a close reading and explication of "A Bird Came Down the Walk"
- To identify the elements that work together in a poem
- To analyze the interdependence of the elements of a poem

TEACHER'S NOTES

THE FACE IN THE MIRROR   *Robert Graves*   Text Page 298

from THE CLOUD   *Percy Bysshe Shelley*   Text Page 300

OBJECTIVES   The aims of this lesson are for the student:

- To identify details in "The Face in the Mirror" that reveal the speaker's past and explain why these details would be called realistic or idealistic
- To interpret the speaker's attitude toward his image in "The Face in the Mirror"
- To cite from "The Face in the Mirror" support for the inference that the speaker's inner man is different from the image in the mirror
- To find the origins of selected words in "The Face in the Mirror" and explain how they came to have their present meanings
- To explain how Shelley attributes purpose and meaning to the actions of the cloud
- To identify the characteristics attributed to the cloud
- To write a paragraph in which the speaker is an animal or object
- To prewrite for subjects for a description

READING/CRITICAL THINKING STRATEGIES

Analyzing the Author's Tone

Before students begin to read "The Face in the Mirror," you might ask them to describe an object in the classroom as though it were a beloved treasure of great sentimental value. Then ask students to describe the same object as though it were a piece of junk in which they had no interest. Encourage students to use the same basic details in both descriptions, but to vary their word choice. Refer students to the discussions of *connotation* and *tone* in the **Literary Terms and Techniques** section. Tell students that as they read this poem, they should decide how best to describe the speaker's tone. How do the connotations of words help them to arrive at their decision? After students have finished their reading, ask them to discuss their findings. You might ask them to replace the words or phrases that have negative connotations with synonyms that are more positive and to discuss the effect of the substitutions.

VOCABULARY   The following words are defined in the glossary:

The Face in the Mirror	jowl (s)	(9)	derision	(11)
orbit (s) (2)	prominent	(9)	presumption	(14)
frenetic (7)	ruddy	(10)	pavilion	(15)

ANSWER KEYS

STUDY GUIDE

The Face in the Mirror   Text Page 298
from The Cloud   Text Page 300

1. The poem takes place at a mirror where someone could shave, perhaps in a bathroom. The speaker is studying his face in the mirror as he is getting ready to shave.
2. He got it from a missile fragment in "old-world fighting."
3. Stanzas 1 and 2 focus on the speaker's outward appearance. Stanza 3 focuses on his inner feelings.

continued ☞

4. The speaker seems to be at least middle-aged. His hair is gray, some teeth are missing, and his forehead is wrinkled.

5. The speaker seems to be "young at heart." He has a "boy's presumption" and idealistic goals. Time has aged his face but not his spirit.

6. The poem's speaker is a cloud.

7. The cloud provides water and shade for the plants and dew to nourish the buds. The cloud also brings hail and thunder.

8. The speaker-cloud is comparing itself to a bird.

9. The mother of the buds is the earth.

10. The speaker appears this way in lines 1–8.

11. The speaker appears this way in lines 9–12.

12. The speaker refers to its laughter as thunder.

13. a. His lips are full and red. His hair is gray and does not lie flat but seems to stick out.
    b. The speaker's face seems asymmetrical since he describes his eye sockets as uneven and one brow as drooping below the other.
    c. Skin hangs down noticeably below the speaker's jaw.
    d. This is a romantic image that suggests an elite, exotic goal.
    e. A boy's presumption or daring might differ from a man's because it has not been tempered by experience, failure, or disappointment.
    f. Displeasure and criticism are expressed.

14. Students' opinions and wording will likely vary somewhat, but most will agree that the speaker-cloud is boastful. The entire poem recounts the cloud's activities and accomplishments.

LANGUAGE SKILLS

The Face in the Mirror   Text Page 298
A. 1. haunted, glaring
   2. drooping
   3. inhering
   4. poised
   5. mirrored

B. 6. V, A
   7. V, A
   8. A, V
   9. V, A
   10. V, A

C. 11. the frightening movie, the frightened audience
   12. some approving voters, the approved measure
   13. some surprising news, our surprised teacher
   14. the interesting events, the interested reporter

15. the amusing incident, my amused classmates

D. Answers will vary. Students' sentences should include the following phrases:
   16. the dented fender
   17. his finished essay
   18. the neglected garden
   19. the lined paper
   20. the corrected sentences
   21. the trumpeting elephant
   22. the darkening clouds
   23. the puzzling ending
   24. our worried mother
   25. the completed survey

BUILDING VOCABULARY

The Face in the Mirror   Text Page 298
Etymologies will vary depending on dictionaries students use.
1. a. *pavilion* [from Latin *papilio,* "butterfly"]
   b. Answers will vary.
2. a. *derision* [from Latin *de–,* pejorative, and *ridere,* "to laugh"]
   b. Students should agree that they would feel hurt and angry.
3. a. *presumption* [from Latin *prae–,* "before," and *sumere,* "to take"]
   b. Answers will vary.
4. a. *frenetic* [from Greek *phrenetikos,* "mad," from phrenitis, "delirium," from *phren,* "mind"]
   b. Answers will vary.
5. a. *prominent* [from Latin *pro–,* "moving forward," and *minere,* "to project"]
   b. A prominent jaw juts forward.
   c. Answers will vary.
6. a. *ruddy* [from Old English *rudu,* "red"]
   b. A person's cheeks, face, complexion; the moon; a blush
7. a. *jowl* [from Old English *ceafl,* "jaw, cheek"]
   b. The jaw or cheek
8. a. *orbit* [from Latin *orbis,* "a circle or wheel"]
   b. The eye
   c. Answers will vary.

SELECTION TEST

The Face in the Mirror   Text Page 298
from The Cloud   Text Page 300
1. c   3. b   5. a   7. b   9. a
2. a   4. d   6. c   8. c   10. c

Study Guide

NAME _____

CLASS _____ DATE _____ SCORE _____

THE FACE IN THE MIRROR *and*
from THE CLOUD   *(Pages 298–300)*

Robert Graves (1895–1985) *and* Percy Bysshe Shelley (1792–1822)

Understanding the Poems

"The Face in the Mirror" (Page 298)

1. Identify the poem's setting and explain the speaker's actions.

_____

_____

_____

_____

2. How did the speaker get the scar over his eye?

_____

_____

_____

3. Which stanzas describe the speaker's outward appearance? Which describe his inward feelings?

_____

_____

_____

4. Outwardly, what is the speaker's approximate age? How do you know?

_____

_____

_____

_____

continued ☞

5. Inwardly, how old does the speaker feel?

_____

_____

_____

from *"The Cloud"* (Page 300)

6. Identify the poem's speaker.

_____

_____

7. List the cloud's activities.

_____

_____

_____

8. To what does the speaker compare itself in line 5 when it refers to "my wings"?

_____

_____

9. Identify the mother of the buds, who dances around the sun (lines 7–8).

_____

_____

10. In which lines does the speaker appear beneficent and loving?

_____

_____

_____

11. In which lines does the speaker appear menacing and destructive?

_____

_____

continued ☞

12. Describe the speaker's laughter.

_____

_____

Understanding Vocabulary

13. Find *orbit(s)* (line 2), *frenetic* (line 7), *jowl(s)* (line 9), *prominent* (line 9), *ruddy* (line 10), *derision* (line 11), *presumption* (line 14), and *pavilion* (line 15) in "The Face in the Mirror" and check their meanings in the glossary or a dictionary. Then answer the following questions:

a. Describe the speaker's lips and hair in your own words. _____

_____

_____

b. Is the speaker's face symmetrical or asymmetrical? Explain your answer. _____

_____

_____

_____

c. Explain the image of "jowls, prominent." _____

_____

_____

d. What kind of image does the poem's last line present? _____

_____

_____

e. Describe how a boy's presumption might differ from that of a man. _____

_____

_____

_____

continued ☞

f. If someone scowls derision, what feelings are expressed?

_____

_____

Writing and Responding to Literature

14. Describe the speaker of "The Cloud." How would you characterize the speaker's personality? Use evidence from the poem to support your ideas.

_____

_____

_____

_____

_____

_____

_____

_____

_____

_____

NAME _____

CLASS _____ DATE _____ SCORE _____

The Face in the Mirror   *Robert Graves*   *(Page 298)*

———— MORE ABOUT PARTICIPLES ————

Adjectives are words that modify nouns. Participles are a special class of adjectives derived, or formed, from verbs. By using different kinds of adjectives, writers enliven their work. As you read the following lines, notice the variety of adjectives (underlined) that Robert Graves uses.

> Crookedly <u>broken</u> nose—<u>low</u> tackling caused it;
> Cheeks, <u>furrowed</u>; <u>coarse</u> <u>gray</u> hair, <u>flying</u> frenetic;
> Forehead, <u>wrinkled</u> and <u>high</u>; *(Page 298, lines 6–8)**

In these lines, the adjective *low* modifies the gerund *tackling;* the adjectives *coarse, gray,* and *frenetic* modify the noun *hair;* and the adjective *high* modifies the noun *forehead.* The lines also include **participles**—verb forms that can be used as adjectives.

EXAMPLES   <u>broken</u> nose   <u>furrowed</u> cheeks

<u>flying</u> hair   <u>wrinkled</u> forehead

Participles are formed from verbs. **Present participles,** such as *flying,* are composed of the plain form of the verb plus *-ing.* **Past participles,** such as *furrowed* and *wrinkled,* are composed of the plain form of the verb plus *-d* or *-ed.* Notice, however, that certain past participles, such as *broken,* are irregularly formed.

   Although they are formed from verbs, participles cannot stand alone as verbs. However, participles may be used with a helping verb (*have* and its various forms or *be* and its various forms) to form a verb phrase.

EXAMPLES   I pause with razor poised, <u>scowl-</u>   [*Scowling* is a participle used as an
                 <u>ing</u> derision   adjective modifying the pronoun *I*.]
              At the mirrored man whose
                 beard needs my attention . . .
                 (lines 11–12)

              The speaker <u>is</u> <u>scowling</u> at his   [*Scowling* is a participle used with a
              face in the mirror.   form of the verb *be* as part of the verb
                                                         phrase.]

* From "The Face in the Mirror" in *Collected Poems 1975* by Robert Graves. Copyright © 1975 by Robert Graves. Reprinted by permission of Oxford University Press, Inc. and A. P. Watt Ltd. on behalf of The Executors of the Estate of Robert Graves.

continued ☞

ACTIVITY A

Underline all of the participles in each of these lines from Graves's poem, found on page 298.*

1. Gray haunted eyes, absentmindedly glaring *(line 1)*

2. . . . one brow drooping/Somewhat over the eye *(lines 2–3)*

3. Because of a missile fragment still inhering, *(line 4)*

4. I pause with razor poised . . . *(line 11)*

5. At the mirrored man whose beard needs my attention, *(line 12)*

ACTIVITY B

Study each of the following pairs of sentences. If the underlined participle is part of the verb, put a **V** in the space provided. If the underlined participle is an adjective, place an **A** in the space.

6. _____ The poem is <u>spoken</u> by a man looking into a mirror.

_____ The <u>spoken</u> words show the poet's amusement with himself.

7. _____ The face in the mirror is <u>aging</u>.

_____ The speaker questions the <u>aging</u> man's presumption.

8. _____ The speaker wonders that the <u>damaged</u> man still thinks about love.

_____ Various forms of combat have <u>damaged</u> the face.

9. _____ The speaker is <u>deriding</u> the face in the mirror.

_____ The <u>deriding</u> tone is softened in the last two lines.

10. _____ The speaker has <u>lost</u> some teeth.

_____ The speaker refers to his <u>lost</u> teeth in the poem.

ACTIVITY C

In the spaces provided, rewrite each of the following clauses as two different phrases. Change the verb in each clause into its present and past participial forms.

EXAMPLE   The wind damaged our treehouse.

_____the damaging wind_____   _____the damaged treehouse_____

---

* From "The Face in the Mirror" in *Collected Poems 1975* by Robert Graves. Copyright © 1975 by Robert Graves. Reprinted by permission of Oxford University Press, Inc. and A. P. Watt Ltd. on behalf of The Executors of the Estate of Robert Graves.

continued ☞

11. The movie frightened the audience.

_____   _____

12. Some voters approved the measure.

_____   _____

13. The news surprised our teacher.

_____   _____

14. The events interested the reporter.

_____   _____

15. The incident amused my classmates.

_____   _____

ACTIVITY D

Change each of the following short clauses into a subject modified by a participle.

    EXAMPLE   His face was smiling.

              His smiling face gave away the secret._____

16. The fender is dented.

_____

_____

17. He finished his essay.

_____

_____

18. The garden has been neglected.

_____

_____

19. The paper is lined.

_____

_____

20. We corrected the sentences.

_____

_____

21. The elephant was trumpeting.

_____

_____

22. The clouds are darkening.

_____

_____

23. The ending puzzles me.

_____

_____

24. Our mother worries about us.

_____

_____

25. We completed the survey.

_____

_____

Building Vocabulary

NAME _____

CLASS _____ DATE _____ SCORE _____

The Face in the Mirror   *Robert Graves*   *(Page 298)*

━━━━━━━━━━━━ **UNDERSTANDING ETYMOLOGIES / APPLYING DEFINITIONS** ━━━━━━━━━━━━

The **etymology** of a word is its history, or the tracing of its development back to its origin. For example, the word *cosmopolitan* comes from the two Greek roots *kosmos* ("world") and *polis* ("city").

In many cases, tracing the etymology of a word provides insight into its meaning. For example, the word *formidable* can be traced through Middle English and Old French back to the Latin word *formidablis,* meaning "to fear or dread," and even further back to the Greek word *mormoros,* meaning "fear." Consequently, a *formidable* opponent is one that causes fear, one that is awesome, impressive, and hard to defeat.

Etymologies are usually given in brackets at the beginning or end of a dictionary entry. An etymology gives the most recent source first and goes backward in time to the original source. Here, for example, is the etymology for *lemon* from *Webster's New World Dictionary:*

[ME. *lymon* < MFr. *limon* < Ar. *laimūn* < Per. *līmūn*]

According to this etymology, *lemon* comes from Middle English *lymon,* which comes from Middle French *limon,* which comes from Arabic *laimūn,* which comes from the Persian *līmūn.*

ACTIVITY

Use a dictionary to find the etymology and meaning(s) of each of the following words. For each word, write the etymology in the space provided, and complete the other items as directed.

1. *pavilion*

   a. ETYMOLOGY _____

   b. Tell what kinds of activities take place in a *pavilion.* _____

   _____

   _____

2. *derision*

   a. ETYMOLOGY _____

   b. Tell how you would feel if someone treated you with *derision.* _____

   _____

   _____

continued ☞

3. *presumption*

    a. ETYMOLOGY _____

    b. Tell about a time when you made a *presumption* that turned out to be incorrect.

    _____

    _____

    _____

    _____

4. *frenetic*

    a. ETYMOLOGY _____

    b. Describe the action of a person you would call *frenetic*. _____

    _____

    _____

    _____

5. *prominent*

    a. ETYMOLOGY _____

    b. Describe a *prominent* jaw. _____

    _____

    _____

    c. Name two *prominent* people in your school, and tell why they are prominent. _____

    _____

    _____

6. *ruddy*

    a. ETYMOLOGY _____

    b. Name two things that could be described as *ruddy*. _____

    _____

continued ☞

7. *jowl*

    a. ETYMOLOGY _____

    b. What part of the body is the *jowl*? _____

_____

8. *orbit*

    a. ETYMOLOGY _____

    b. In anatomy, with what body part is the *orbit* associated? _____

    c. Would you like to be part of a space expedition *orbiting* the earth? Why or why not.

_____

_____

_____

_____

_____

POETRY

The Speaker   (*Page 298*)

AN OPEN-BOOK TEST

Understanding Poetry. Write the letter of the *best* answer to each question. (10 points each)

1. In "The Face in the Mirror," we find that the face shows all of the following features *except*
   - **a.** a crooked nose
   - **b.** gray hair
   - **c.** straight teeth
   - **d.** full lips

   1. _____

2. In the poem, what is the speaker doing?
   - **a.** Looking in a mirror
   - **b.** Talking to a friend
   - **c.** Riding in a car
   - **d.** Looking at a picture

   2. _____

3. The tone, or attitude, of Graves' poem is which of the following?
   - **a.** Impersonal or indifferent
   - **b.** Self-critical
   - **c.** Egotistical and self-satisfied
   - **d.** Boastful

   3. _____

4. Graves' poem possesses all of the following *except*
   - **a.** approximate rhyme
   - **b.** stanzas
   - **c.** complete sentences
   - **d.** formal, flowery language

   4. _____

5. The first two stanzas describe the face; what does the third stanza do?
   - **a.** Questions the speaker's feelings
   - **b.** Comments on the features of the face
   - **c.** Derides the handsome features
   - **d.** Addresses the queen

   5. _____

6. The speaker in "The Cloud" says that it helps all of the following *except* one. Which one?
   - **a.** Flowers
   - **b.** Leaves
   - **c.** Seas
   - **d.** Buds

   6. _____

7. The speaker brings, among other things,
   - **a.** wind, rain, and hail
   - **b.** shade, dew, and hail
   - **c.** streams, hail, and rain
   - **d.** hail, dew, and seas

   7. _____

8. One physical feature of the speaker is its
   - **a.** flail
   - **b.** dreams
   - **c.** wings
   - **d.** laughter

   8. _____

9. The main division in the poem is between
   - **a.** good weather and bad
   - **b.** dreams and reality
   - **c.** light and shade
   - **d.** earth and water

   9. _____

10. The speaker's tone is mostly
    - **a.** apologetic
    - **b.** threatening
    - **c.** boastful
    - **d.** intellectual

    10. _____

TEACHER'S NOTES

TO SATCH	*Samuel Allen (Paul Vesey)*	Text Page 302
CARGOES	*John Masefield*	Text Page 304
DREAM DEFERRED	*Langston Hughes*	Text Page 306

OBJECTIVES

The aims of this lesson are for the student:
- To identify the speaker of "To Satch" and support the identification
- To find evidence in "To Satch" of the speaker's self-confidence and sense of humor
- To evaluate the appropriateness of the language used in "To Satch"
- To identify the historical periods implied by the descriptions of the ships in stanzas 2 and 3 of "Cargoes"
- To compare the ships and their cargoes
- To infer, from the description of the cargoes, differences between past times and present times
- To describe the poet's attitude toward the third ship, supporting the description with words from the poem
- To demonstrate recognition of connotation and the effect of its use
- To evaluate the effectiveness of the poetic use of comparisons in "Dream Deferred"
- To identify the words with connotative meanings and explain the effect of their use in "Dream Deferred"
- To write a composition comparing the diction of "Dream Deferred" and "Cargoes"

READING/CRITICAL THINKING STRATEGIES

Analyzing the Use of Language

Before students begin reading "To Satch," ask them to give some examples of language that they consider to be poetic. Then ask them to discuss how popular sports figures use language. Do students see any poetic potential in that language? Tell students that as they read this poem they should consider what language seems to them to be specifically poetic and what language seems to be ordinary speech. After students have completed their reading, ask them to compare their findings. What can make ordinary speech poetic?

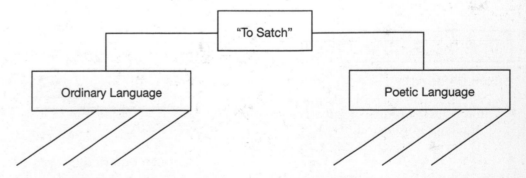

VOCABULARY

Dream Deferred
Fester (line 4) is defined in the glossary.

continued ☞

ANSWER KEYS

STUDY GUIDE A

To Satch   **Text Page 302**
Cargoes   **Text Page 304**

1. The speaker is Satchel Paige.
2. The speaker feels as if he will never stop pitching. He will go on until he dies and then continue even in heaven.
3. God
4. The third stanza contrasts most sharply with the other two. Stanzas 1 and 2 are similar in diction and feeling, but stanza 3 is distinctly different.
5. The speaker's attitude toward these ships is romantic.
6. The cargo of these ships is rare, exotic, expensive, and luxurious.
7. The cargo described in the third stanza is cheap, dirty, utilitarian, and industrial.
8. The poem's diction is informal. The poet uses baseball slang such as *whip* for *throw* in line 6. (Students' examples will vary.)
9. **a.** Ivory suggests the unusual, the expensive.
   b. Diamonds suggest beauty, perhaps love.
   c. Coal suggests work, dirt, industry.
10. *Sweet, gold,* and *cheap* are the adjectives. The first two adjectives have positive meanings and connotations. The last adjective has negative connotations. It clearly shows the lack of beauty and luxury in the third ship.
11. Students' opinions will vary, but most will see this tendency to idealize the past, emphasizing the good parts and neglecting the bad, as part of human nature. They might cite examples from their own experience or from movies or television or their reading.

STUDY GUIDE B

Dream Deferred   **Text Page 306**

1. A deferred dream is a goal or hope or ambition that is frustrated or put off or postponed. (Students' wording will vary.)
2. (1) *Dry up,* (2) *fester,* (3) *stink,* (4) *crust* and *sugar,* (5) *sag,* (6) *explode*
3. **a.** It would fade or wither or grow smaller.
   b. It would become a burden.
   c. It would cause trouble or destruction.
4. The poem's images are powerful but ugly and unpleasant.
5. The poem does not answer the question directly. However, all the possibilities raised in the poem are negative or ugly. The implication

seems to be that whatever happens, the result will be ugly.
6. "To form pus" is the denotative meaning within the poem's context. The poem's image is literally of an infected sore. "To grow embittered" is an appropriate connotative meaning because a person whose hopes are frustrated may become bitter and hateful as a result.
7. Most students will see "Dream Deferred" as down-to-earth and realistic. To support their opinion, they might cite the poem's imagery, which is powerful but ugly and unpleasant, or the poem's theme, which certainly paints a grim reality. Hughes is saying that if hopes are stifled, there can be many consequences, none of them pleasant and some even dangerous.

LANGUAGE SKILLS

Cargoes   **Text Page 304**

A. 1. diamonds, emeralds, amethysts, topazes,
   2. Ophir, galleon,
   3. Bakery, stable, saloon,
   4. poetry, drama,
   5. no commas needed

B. 6. novels, flute,
   7. James, Marcie,
   8. sugar, flour,
   9. hamburgers, french fries,
   10. hours, history,

C. 11. seeds, plants,
   12. dish; dish;
   13. Channel, Everest,
   14. subject; subject;
   15. college, psychology

D. 16.–20. Answers will vary.

SELECTION TEST

To Satch   **Text Page 302**
Cargoes   **Text Page 304**
Dream Deferred   **Text Page 306**

A. 1. b   5. d
    2. d   6. b
    3. a   7. d
    4. d   8. a

B. 9. a   11. c
   10. b   12. a

Study Guide
A

NAME _____

CLASS _____ DATE _____ SCORE _____

TO SATCH *and* CARGOES   *(Pages 302–304)*

Samuel Allen (1917–) *and* John Masefield (1878–1967)

Understanding the Poems

"To Satch" (Page 302)

1. Identify the poem's speaker.

_____

2. What does the speaker feel he will never stop doing?

_____

_____

_____

3. Who observes the speaker's heavenly performance?

_____

"Cargoes" (Page 304)

4. This poem relies upon contrast. Identify which of the three stanzas contrasts most sharply with the other two.

_____

_____

_____

5. Describe the speaker's attitude toward the ships described in stanzas 1 and 2.

_____

_____

6. Characterize the cargo held in the ships of stanzas 1 and 2.

_____

_____

continued ☞

7. Characterize the cargo held in the ship of stanza 3.

_____

_____

Understanding Literary Elements

8. Is the diction of "To Satch" formal or informal? Give an example to support your opinion.

_____

_____

_____

Understanding Vocabulary

9. What are the connotations of each word listed below?

a. *ivory* _____

b. *diamonds* _____

c. *coal* _____

10. The last line of each stanza includes an adjective. Name these adjectives and explain how they establish the difference between the first two ships and the last ship.

_____

_____

_____

Writing and Responding to Literature

11. In "Cargoes," John Masefield idealizes the past at the expense of the present. Do you think this is a common tendency of human nature? Use an example from your experience or reading to support your answer.

_____

_____

_____

_____

DREAM DEFERRED   *(Page 306)*

Langston Hughes (1902–1967)

Understanding the Poem

1. In your own words, explain the meaning of a deferred dream.

_____

_____

_____

2. The poem is based on the initial question and offers six possible answers. List the six verbs, in their order, that are the six things the deferred dream might do.

_____

_____

3. In your own words, explain what a deferred dream would do if it

    a. dried up (line 2): _____

    b. sagged "like a heavy load" (lines 9–10): _____

    c. exploded (line 11): _____

4. What connotations are associated with the poem's images?

_____

_____

5. Does the poem answer the question asked in the first line? If so, what is the answer? If not, what assumptions about an answer can be made?

_____

_____

_____

_____

Understanding Vocabulary

6. Find *fester* in line 4 of "Dream Deferred." *Fester* can mean either "to form pus" or "to grow embittered." Explain how both of these meanings are appropriate within the context of the poem.

_____

_____

_____

_____

Writing and Responding to Literature

7. Hughes's biography (page 307) calls his work "down-to-earth and realistic." Is this an accurate description of "Dream Deferred"? Give specific evidence from the poem to support your opinion.

_____

_____

_____

_____

_____

_____

_____

_____

Language Skills	NAME _____
	CLASS _____ DATE _____ SCORE _____

Cargoes *John Masefield* (Page 304)

─────────────── **ITEMS IN A SERIES** ───────────────

Writers use commas to present their images and ideas more clearly to readers. Notice John Masefield's use of commas to separate similar items in the following lines from his poem.

> Dirty British coaster with a salt-caked smokestack,
> Butting through the Channel in the mad March days,
> With a cargo of Tyne coal,
> Road rails, pig lead,
> Firewood, ironware, and cheap tin trays.   *(Page 304, lines 11-15)*

A **series** is three or more items written one after another. The items in a series may be words, phrases, or clauses. When you have a series of similar items, use commas to separate them from one another. The number of commas in a series is one less than the number of items in the series.

EXAMPLES   The ship carried a cargo of Tyne coal, **[Series of Nouns]**
road rails, pig lead, firewood, ironware,
and cheap tin trays.

The gulls were on the pier, near the **[Series of Phrases]**
beach, and in the air.

The crew lifted the anchor, the ship sailed, **[Series of Short Clauses]**
and the crowd cheered.

ACTIVITY A

Insert commas wherever they are needed in each of the following sentences. Some sentences will not need commas.

1. There was also a stately Spanish galleon with a cargo of diamonds emeralds amethysts topazes and cinnamon.

2. Masefield saw three ships—a Quinquireme from Ophir a stately Spanish galleon and a dirty British coaster.

3. Masefield supported himself through a variety of jobs: working in a bakery a livery stable a saloon and a carpet mill.

4. His work includes poetry drama and novels.

5. The sights he saw and the experiences he underwent made him want to read and write poetry.

continued ☞

ACTIVITY B

Insert commas wherever they are needed in each of the following sentences.

6. Martha's hobbies include reading novels playing the flute and working in her garden.

7. James Marcie and Fred are all running for class president.

8. The recipe calls for a cup of brown sugar two cups of flour and one teaspoon of baking soda.

9. We ordered hamburgers french fries and milkshakes to go.

10. After studying for two hours writing an essay for history and mowing the lawn, I was exhausted.

Special Cases of Items in a Series

Some writers leave out the comma between the last two items in a series.

> EXAMPLE   The salad contained macaroni, tomatoes, onions, lettuce and olives.

It is good practice, however, to develop the habit of using the last comma before the word *and* to prevent confusion.

> CONFUSING: Charles, Mary and I will do the shopping for the party.

> CLEAR: Charles, Mary, and I will do the shopping for the party.

The first sentence is confusing because it is not clear whether Charles is being addressed or is going with the others. It is clear in the second sentence that all three of them will do the shopping. To avoid confusion, develop the habit of using the last comma before the *and* that joins the final two items in a series. Use semicolons to separate items in a series if the items contain commas.

> EXAMPLE   We are voting for John, who is a good student; Mary, who has experience; and Sammy, who is hard-working.

ACTIVITY C

Add needed commas or semicolons to each of the following sentences.

11. Planting the seeds tending the new plants and harvesting the large fruit are some of the joys of gardening.

12. Janet brought lasagna, an Italian dish tacos, a Mexican dish and hot dogs, an American dish.

13. Swimming the English Channel climbing Mt. Everest and sky diving are three popular daredevil sports.

continued ☞

14. I received good grades in algebra, which is my hardest subject English, which is my favorite subject and Spanish, which is my easiest subject.

15. When I finish school, I want to attend college earn a degree in psychology and work in the field of child care.

ACTIVITY D

In the space provided, write sentences that use each of the following parts of speech in a series. Remember that a series consists of three or more items.

16. adjectives: _____

_____

17. nouns: _____

_____

18. pronouns: _____

_____

19. verbs: _____

_____

20. adverbs: _____

_____

NAME _____

CLASS _____ DATE _____ SCORE _____

Diction   *(Page 302)*

A. Understanding Poetry.   Write the letter of the *best* answer to each question.
(*10 points each*)

1. In "To Satch," the speaker is
   a. the poet himself
   b. Satchel Paige
   c. an unidentified baseball player
   d. an athletic-minded angel   1. _____

2. This poem involves a number of implied, unanswered questions. Which of
   the following questions *is* answered?
   a. How does Satch get to heaven?
   b. How does he manage to grab stars?
   c. Whom does he strike out?
   d. Who observes his performance?   2. _____

3. In "Cargoes," the poet gives us an abbreviated history of
   a. shipping   **c.** human beings
   b. exploration   **d.** commerce   3. _____

4. Vivid contrasts are almost the essence of "Cargoes." Which of the following
   contrasts is *not* contained in the poem?
   a. Long ago—the present day   **c.** Romantic—ordinary
   b. Costly—cheap   **d.** Wanted—unwanted   4. _____

5. Which of the following may be found in "Cargoes"?
   a. Uniform line length
   b. Stanzas of different kinds
   c. Complete sentences
   d. An "out-of-sight" speaker   5. _____

6. "Dream Deferred" can *best* be described as a poem about
   a. lazy people
   b. frustrated hopes
   c. people who daydream
   d. the brevity and cruelty of life   6. _____

7. All of the following correctly paraphrase words or phrases in "Dream
   Deferred" *except*
   a. "dream" (line 1): a hope or aspiration
   b. "dry up" (line 2): wither or fade
   c. "sags like a heavy load" (lines 9–10): becomes too burdensome
   d. "explode" (line 11): vanish like smoke   7. _____

8. "Dream Deferred" contains all of the following *except*
   a. regular stanzas   **c.** questions
   b. several comparisons   **d.** inversion   8. _____

continued ☞

B. Comparing Poems.   The following questions ask you to compare the subject matter and poetic techniques of these three poems. An answer may be used more than once. (*5 points each*)

    a. "To Satch"   **c.** "Dream Deferred"

    b. "Cargoes"   **d.** None of these poems

  9. Which poem is an admiring, humorous tribute?   9. _____

10. Which poem contains contrasting images?   10. _____

11. Which poem depends on questions?   11. _____

12. Which poem avoids rhyme altogether?   12. _____

TEACHER'S NOTES

OUR HOUSE IN HADONG
Wendy Wilder Larsen and Tran Thi Nga   Text Page 308

THE MEADOW MOUSE
Theodore Roethke   Text Page 310

THE FAWN   *Edna St. Vincent Millay*   Text Page 312

OBJECTIVES
The aims of this lesson are for the student:
- To evaluate the imagery in "Our House in Hadong"
- To analyze the speaker's attitude about her home in "Our House in Hadong"
- To identify the literary device *simile* in "Our House in Hadong"
- To identify the comparisons used in "The Meadow Mouse" to describe the mouse
- To infer how the speaker feels toward the mouse in "The Meadow Mouse"
- To identify images of helplessness and terror in "The Meadow Mouse"
- To explain how the speakers in "The Meadow Mouse" express compassion for all helpless creatures
- To analyze the word structure of words selected from "The Meadow Mouse"
- To tell how the speaker felt and how she describes what she saw in "The Fawn"
- To interpret selected words used by the speaker in "The Fawn"
- To freewrite on several subjects for a description

VOCABULARY
The Meadow Mouse
Absurd (line 7) and *nuzzle(d)* (line 22) are defined in the glossary.

The Fawn
Retrieve (line 2) and *cleft* (line 5) are defined in the glossary.

ANSWER KEYS

STUDY GUIDE A

Our House in Hadong   Text Page 308
The Meadow Mouse   Text Page 310

1. She thinks it was their best house. She was very happy there.
2. The jackfruit was too rich for their climate.
3. They had everything they needed except beef and rice.
4. They would drain the big pond and catch the butter fish. They had a cookout on the tiny island, and when the moon came up they'd watch goldfish move into warm water. They would listen to night noises and remember the jungle sounds.
5. The mouse has escaped and presumably returned to the wild.

6. In spite of the speaker's hopes and kindness, the mouse still feared and distrusted him.
7. They are all natural predators of the mouse.
8. All are helpless creatures in life-threatening circumstances.
9. a. *Cartoon*
   b. This image reflects a feeling of protection and affection.
10. Students' wording and opinions may vary but may include some of the following observations about the speaker: (1) He is observant: He describes the mouse in detail (whiskers, feet, and ears) and uses comparisons. (2) He is hopeful: He hopes the mouse no longer fears him. (3) He is caring: He provides food, water, and shelter for the mouse and tries to rescue it from its

continued ☞

hostile environment. (4) He is realizes what the odds are for the mouse's survival. (5) He is compassionate: He thinks of other helpless creatures and feels sorry for them.

STUDY GUIDE B

The Fawn   Text Page 312

1. The speaker unexpectedly comes upon a fawn asleep on a bed of moss in the woods.

2. The fawn was not taking advantage of its natural camouflage and was not blending into its surroundings for protection.

3. The speaker wishes for the fawn's acceptance because she knows that she cannot expect its love.

4. The speaker wishes that she might become a branch or a root of the tree by which the fawn sleeps. Then, she would blend into the fawn's environment and go unnoticed.

5. *Jerked, crashing, leaping,* and *stumbling* suggest hurried, frantic movement.

6. **a.** Her experience of coming upon a fawn alone in the wild was very rare, a once-in-a-lifetime experience that she will always remember but never duplicate.

   b. The fawn has small, shiny black split hooves.

7. I would have paid more than I care to admit to a thrifty person if I could have had the fawn as my friend for just a moment in the forest. (Students' wording will vary.)

8. The speaker feels protective toward the fawn. She sees it as vulnerable, asleep in the open in the woods, and refers to it as a child. The speaker sees the fawn as beautiful and extraordinary. She says that it is hard to believe that she ever saw it. She uses words such as *polished* and *ebony* to suggest the fawn's beauty and special quality. The speaker wishes to have a relationship with the fawn, to have its acceptance,

to be its friend; but by using *might,* she indicates that she knows this wish is impossible in spite of her wonder and protective feelings.

LANGUAGE SKILLS

The Meadow Mouse   Text Page 310
A. 1. like a cartoon-mouse
   2. from his bottle-cap watering trough
   3. under him
   4. in my palm
   5. toward the least sound

B. into the deep grass, in the dusty rubble, in the tub

C. 6.–8. Each phrase can be moved only to the beginning of the sentence without changing the meaning of the sentence.
   9.–10. The phrase can be moved to the end of the sentence.

BUILDING VOCABULARY

Dream Deferred   Text Page 306
The Meadow Mouse   Text Page 310
The Fawn   Text Page 312
Wording of definitions will vary. The following are suggested definitions. Sentences will also vary.

1. *fester:* become infected; develop pus
2. *absurd:* ridiculous
3. *nuzzled:* pushed or rubbed with the nose; snuggled
4. *retrieved:* brought back
5. *cleft:* split
6. *deferred:* put off; postponed
7. *dappled:* spotted

NAME _____

CLASS _____ DATE _____ SCORE _____

OUR HOUSE IN HADONG *and*
THE MEADOW MOUSE

(Pages 308–311)

Wendy Wilder Larsen *and* **Tran Thi Nga**
Theodore Roethke (1908–1963)

Understanding the Poems

"Our House in Hadong" *(Pages 308–309)*

1. How does the speaker feel about the house and land she describes?

   _____

   _____

2. Why did the speaker's father prevent the children from eating the jackfruit?

   _____

   _____

3. What items could the family neither raise nor make?

   _____

   _____

4. What happened each New Year?

   _____

   _____

   _____

   _____

"The Meadow Mouse" *(Pages 310–311)*

5. Explain what has happened in Part I.

   _____

   _____

   _____

continued ☞

6. What seems to be the mouse's reaction to the speaker in lines 1–16?

_____

_____

7. If the mouse no longer trembled when the speaker approached it (lines 17–19), what might this indicate?

_____

_____

_____

8. What images in Part I create a mood or feeling of playfulness or affection?

_____

_____

_____

9. What does the speaker discover in Part II?

_____

_____

_____

10. What does the mouse's action in Part II suggest about its feelings toward the speaker?

_____

_____

_____

11. What do the hawk, the owl, the snake, and the tomcat have in common?

_____

_____

12. What does the mouse have in common with the images of the nestling, the turtle, and the paralytic in lines 26–28?

_____

_____

Understanding Vocabulary

13. Find *absurd* (line 7) and *nuzzle(d)* (line 22) in "The Meadow Mouse" and check their meanings in the glossary or a dictionary. Then answer the following questions:

a. What is the best context clue for *absurd* in line 7? _____

_____

b. What feeling does the image in line 22 reflect? _____

_____

_____

Writing and Responding to Literature

14. Describe the speaker of "The Meadow Mouse." What type of person is he? Use specific details from the poem to support your opinion.

_____

_____

_____

_____

_____

_____

_____

_____

_____

_____

_____

Study Guide B

THE FAWN   (Pages 312–313)

Edna St. Vincent Millay (1892–1950)

Understanding the Poem

1. Describe the poem's setting.

   _____

   _____

2. Why would the fawn's mother never have advised him to sleep on the moss?

   _____

   _____

   _____

   _____

3. For what does the speaker wish in lines 14–15?

   _____

   _____

   _____

4. In order not to surprise or startle the fawn, what two things does the speaker wish that she might become?

   _____

   _____

   _____

   _____

5. What words or images in the final stanza suggest the fawn's sense of alarm?

   _____

   _____

continued ☞

Understanding Vocabulary

6. Find *retrieve* (line 2) and *cleft* (line 5) in the poem and check their meanings in the glossary or a dictionary. Then answer the following questions:

   a. Why won't the speaker be able to retrieve the experience she describes? _____

   _____

   _____

   _____

   b. In your own words, describe the fawn's feet. _____

   _____

   _____

Understanding Literary Elements

7. In "The Fawn," the poet uses inverted word order in lines 11–13. What would be the usual word order?

   _____

   _____

   _____

Writing and Responding to Literature

8. How does the speaker feel about the fawn? Support your opinion with details from the poem.

   _____

   _____

   _____

   _____

   _____

   _____

   _____

Language
Skills

NAME _____

CLASS _____ DATE _____ SCORE_____

The Meadow Mouse   *Theodore Roethke*   *(Page 310)*

───────────────────────────── **ADVERB PHRASES** ─────────────────────────────

Writers can use prepositional phrases to tell *when, where, how, how much,* or *how far.* As you read this excerpt from "The Meadow Mouse," notice Theodore Roethke's use of prepositional phrases to give this kind of information.

> In a shoe box stuffed in an old nylon stocking
> Sleeps the baby mouse I found in the meadow,
> Where he trembled and shook beneath a stick
> Till I caught him by the tail and brought him in,
> Cradled in my hand, *(Page 310, lines 1–5)*

A **prepositional phrase** is a group of words that begins with a preposition—a word like *in, by, under,* or *beneath*—and ends with a noun or a pronoun. Prepositional phrases may be used in sentences as adverbs or adjectives. An **adverbial prepositional phrase** or **adverb phrase** tells *when, where, how, how much,* or *how far* and is used as an adverb. In the lines quoted above, five of the six underlined phrases tell *where.* The phrase *by the tail* tells *how* the speaker picked up the mouse. An adverb phrase may modify a verb, an adjective, or an adverb.

EXAMPLES	So much he just lies in one cor-ner *(line 13)*	**[The adverb phrase modifies the verb *lies* and tells *where*.]**
	Whitish and spread wide when he tried to struggle away, Wriggling like a miniscule puppy. *(lines 10–11)*	**[The adverb phrase modifies the participle *wriggling*, which is used as an an adjective. The phrase tells *how*.]**
	When I come close to him? *(line 18)*	**[The adverb phrase modifies the adverb *close* and tells *where*.]**

ACTIVITY A

Underline each of the adverb phrases in the following lines. Remember that not all prepositional phrases are adverb phrases.

1. His absurd whiskers sticking out like a cartoon-mouse, *(Page 310, line 7)*

2. Now he's eaten his three kinds of cheese and drunk from
    his bottle-cap watering-trough— *(Page 310, lines 12)*

3. His tail curled under him, . . . *(Page 311, line 14)*

4. Where has he gone, my meadow mouse,/My thumb of a child that nuzzled in my
    palm?— *(Page 311, lines 21–22)*

5. . . . his batlike ears/Twitching, tilting toward the least sound. *(Page 311, lines 15–16)*

continued ☞

ACTIVITY B

Underline all of the adverb phrases in the following passage.

> . . . the nestling fallen into the deep grass,
> The turtle gasping in the dusty rubble of the highway,
> The paralytic stunned in the tub, and the water rising—
> All things innocent, hapless, forsaken. *(Page 311, lines 26–29)*

ACTIVITY C

An adverb phrase can often be placed in more than one position in a sentence. Rewrite each of the following sentences, placing each adverb phrase in a different position. Do not change the meaning of the sentence.

EXAMPLE   The owl watches for prey from the elm tree.

From the elm tree, the owl watches for prey.
_____

6. The field mouse nuzzled in the speaker's palm.

_____

_____

7. The speaker found the baby mouse in the meadow.

_____

_____

8. The mouse was trembling beneath a stick.

_____

_____

9. In his secure shoe box, the mouse ate and drank and slept.

_____

_____

10. During its stay in the house, the speaker imagined that the mouse became less afraid.

_____

_____

Building Vocabulary

Dream Deferred	*Langston Hughes*	*(Page 306)*
The Meadow Mouse	*Theodore Roethke*	*(Page 310)*
The Fawn	*Edna St. Vincent Millay*	*(Page 312)*

————————— **USING CONTEXT CLUES / USING WORDS IN CONTEXT** —————————

Sometimes you can guess the meaning of an unfamiliar word from its **context**—the words, phrases, and sentences that surround it. The context may provide an example, a definition, or some other clue to the word's meaning.

ACTIVITY

In each of the following numbered items, use the context clues to guess the meaning of the italicized word. Then, without consulting any source, write a definition for the italicized word. Check your guesses in a dictionary or in the glossary in the textbook. Finally, write an original sentence using the italicized word correctly.

1. That cat scratch may become infected and *fester,* so you had better go wash it and put an antiseptic on it right away.

   MEANING _____

   SENTENCE _____

   _____

2. Jeanne was joking when she made the *absurd* statement that, given the right wind, she was sure she could fly.

   MEANING _____

   SENTENCE _____

   _____

3. When he finished combing and brushing the horse, it always *nuzzled* his cheek, as if in thanks.

   MEANING _____

   SENTENCE _____

   _____

continued ☞

4. Allison *retrieved* the tennis balls that her brother had hit over the fence.

MEANING _____

SENTENCE _____

_____

5. Cows and sheep have *cleft* hooves, but horses do not.

MEANING _____

SENTENCE _____

_____

6. In January, she received a letter saying that the admissions committee had *deferred* until April their decision on whether or not to admit her.

MEANING _____

SENTENCE _____

_____

7. The horse's white coat was *dappled* with patches of black.

MEANING _____

SENTENCE _____

_____

TEACHER'S NOTES

WITHOUT TITLE   *Diane Glancy*   Text Page 314
THE SPACE   *Gary Soto*   Text Page 315

OBJECTIVES   The aims of this lesson are for the student:
- To understand the literary devices *simile* and *metaphor* in "Without Title"
- To understand the speaker's attitude in "Without Title"
- To analyze and evaluate the title of "Without Title"
- To make inferences about the location of "The Space"
- To analyze "The Space" for sense imagery, citing examples of images that appeal to each of the five senses
- To suggest what "lessons" the bird might be teaching in "The Space"
- To explain the purpose of using repetition in "The Space"
- To draw inferences about the speaker's feelings in "The Space"

READING/CRITICAL THINKING STRATEGIES

Analyzing the Use of Language

Before students begin to read "The Space," you might refer them to the definition of *imagery* in the **Literary Terms and Techniques** section. Ask students to consider some images they might use to create a picture of a sunny spring day. You may want to have students create a contrasting set of images (a stormy spring day or a winter's day). Remind students that poetry relies heavily on images. Ask them to make careful note of the imagery in Soto's poem. You might ask students to classify the imagery based on which senses are affected. After students have completed their reading, ask them to share their findings and to consider the impact of the imagery on the reader.

Image	Sensory Appeal
hammock . . . among avocado trees, cane, spider-grass	sight

ANSWER KEYS

STUDY GUIDE

Without Title   Text Page 314
The Space   Text Page 315

1. When he brought home horns and hides, she told him to get rid of them.
2. The speaker is more influenced.
3. buffalo, shaman, arrow, bow string
4. Answers will vary, but students may mention the following: identity, ceremony, vision, respect, traditions.

5. Her father was so unified with the buffalo that his night sounds resembled a snore, but were actually buffalo sounds.
6. The speaker's sleeping outside in a hammock and the vegetation, such as cork, banana, and avocado trees, suggest a warm climate.
7. (1) the cocks' gabble (line 12), (2) the grasses' rustle (line 21), and (3) the bird's coo (line 25)
8. Such smells would be intermingled or blended together.

continued ☞

9. The space between trees when the sun rises seems to be the space referred to in the title. It could also be the location itself.

10. Students' answers will vary but should include some or all of the following observations. The speaker values the following: (1) The space's peace: The speaker is literally at rest here but the images themselves also suggest peace. (2) The natural surroundings: All the images are natural ones of vegetation and animal sounds. (3) The solitude of the space: The speaker indicates that the space is out of town and thus away from people. The speaker is also sure that any sounds are made by animals and not people (lines 20–23).

SELECTION TEST

A. 1. c   4. a
    2. d   5. b
    3. b   6. a

B. 7. c   9. a
    8. b   10. d

Study Guide

WITHOUT TITLE and THE SPACE

(Pages 314-315)

Diane Glancy (1941–   ) and Gary Soto (1952–   )

Understanding the Poems

"Without Title" (Page 314)

1. In what ways can you tell that the speaker's mother did not appreciate her husband's heritage?

_____

_____

_____

2. Who is more influenced by his father's loss?

_____

_____

_____

3. What tangible things did the speaker's father lose?

_____

_____

_____

4. What intangible things do you think the speaker's father has lost?

_____

_____

_____

_____

_____

continued ☞

5. What do the lines ". . . and in the night I heard/his buffalo grunts like a snore," mean?

_____

_____

_____

_____

"The Space" (Page 315)

6. What details indicate that "the space" is located in a warm climate?

_____

_____

_____

_____

7. Identify three of the poem's details that appeal to the sense of hearing.

_____

_____

_____

8. Explain what the speaker means by smells that "braid like rope" (line 19).

_____

_____

_____

_____

9. Identify the space in the title of the poem.

_____

_____

_____

continued ☞

Writing and Responding to Literature

10. What do you think the speaker of "The Space" values about his private space? Use details from the poem to support your observations.

_____

_____

_____

_____

_____

_____

_____

_____

_____

_____

┌─────────────┐
│ Selection   │
│ Test   │
└─────────────┘

Imagery   *(Page 308)*

AN OPEN-BOOK TEST

A. Understanding Poetry.   Write the letter of the *best* answer to each question.
(*10 points each*)

1. In "The Meadow Mouse," the speaker expresses a variety of feelings. Which of the following lines is *incorrectly* matched with a mood or feeling?
   a. Line 20: astonishment   **c.** Line 5: pity
   b. Line 7: amusement   **d.** Line 28: horror   1. _____

2. The division of "The Meadow Mouse" into two parts is matched by parallel shifts of mood or contrasts. Which of the following is *not* one of these contrasts or shifts?
   a. Playfulness and helplessness
   b. Humor and seriousness
   c. Hope and despair
   d. Concern and indifference   2. _____

3. "The Fawn" is based on all of the following facts *except* one. Which one?
   a. The poet comes upon a tiny fawn in the woods.
   b. Its mother has just been killed by hunters.
   c. The fawn is not well hidden from view.
   d. It panics and runs off through the trees.   3. _____

4. The speaker in "The Fawn" wishes for the fawn's
   a. acceptance
   b. love
   c. mother to return
   d. willingness to let her pet him   4. _____

5. In "Without Title," the animal that the speaker linked with her father was the
   a. pony
   b. buffalo
   c. wolf
   d. eagle   5. _____

6. In "The Space," the speaker's attitude toward his subject is that of
   a. appreciation   **c.** distaste
   b. puzzlement   **d.** envy   6. _____

7. The poet tells us that it is enough to
   a. feel the water   **c.** be in the natural world
   b. see the geese   **d.** have companions   7. _____

continued ☞

B. Comparing Poems. The following questions ask you to compare the subject matter and poetic techniques of several poems. An answer may be used more than once. *(10 points each)*

    a. "The Meadow Mouse"
    b. "The Fawn"
    c. "Our House in Hadong"
    d. "The Space"
    e. "Without Title"

8. Which poem gives us a vivid picture of the power of the instinct of self-preservation?   8. _____

9. Which poem examines the impersonal cruelty and mercilessness of the world?   9. _____

10. Which poem shows enjoyment of nature for its own sake?   10. _____

THE DAY IS DONE *Henry Wadsworth Longfellow*   Text Page 319

I'LL TELL YOU HOW THE SUN ROSE
Emily Dickinson   Text Page 321

OBJECTIVES   The aims of this lesson are for the student:

- To identify the mood of the speaker in "The Day Is Done" and what it is that he believes can change it
- To identify the two kinds of poetry the speaker refers to in "The Day Is Done" and explain how their music differs
- To analyze the relationship between the opening and concluding stanzas of "The Day Is Done"
- To evaluate the effectiveness of the closing stanzas of "The Day Is Done"
- To identify similes in "The Day Is Done" and explain the comparison in each one
- To identify the referents of key words, such as *news* in line 4 of "I'll Tell You How the Sun Rose"
- To analyze the use of colors in "I'll Tell You How the Sun Rose," and to draw inferences about the sun from these colors
- To interpret the metaphor in line 5 of "I'll Tell You How the Sun Rose," "The hills untied their bonnets"
- To differentiate between *expected word order* and *inverted word order*
- To identify changes in meaning accomplished by the inversion of standard word order in "I'll Tell You How the Sun Rose"
- To describe and relate one's response to poetic images, like the image in line 2 of "I'll Tell You How the Sun Rose"

VOCABULARY   The following words are defined in the glossary:

The Day Is Done	martial	(21)	devoid	(30)
waft (ed) (3)	endeavor	(23)	infest	(42)

ANSWER KEYS

STUDY GUIDE

The Day Is Done   Text Page 319
I'll Tell You How the Sun Rose   Text Page 321

1. It is early evening, and it is raining. The speaker is near the village, perhaps at home.
2. The complete analogy is: sadness and longing : sorrow :: mist : rain.
3. This analogy suggests that the speaker's sadness and longing are not profound or deep. Rather, it suggests the speaker may be feeling a little depressed or weary.
4. The speaker requests an uncomplicated poem telling a story.
5. The poem will calm the speaker's restlessness and take his mind off his worries.
6. Sunrise appears more rapidly according to the speaker.
7. Students' examples will vary.
8. a. Slowly
   b. Mars was the god of war.
   c. The grand old masters' poetry contains themes of life's constant and never-ending work and effort.

continued ☞

d. According to the speaker, the humbler poet works long and hard during the day. The poet's nights hold no rest or relaxation.

   e. *Infest* usually has negative connotations and is associated with something harmful or bothersome.

9. A simile is a figure of speech that compares two unlike things and uses a word such as *like* or *as*.

10. The onset of darkness is compared to the falling of a feather: Both descend slowly and gently.

11. Cares are compared to Arabs. Both leave quietly.

12. A metaphor is a figure of speech that directly compares two unlike things, saying one thing is another. It differs from a simile, which says one thing is *like* or *as* another.

13. Here the bands of color at sunrise are compared to strips of colorful ribbon.

14. Line 4

15. Both poems use figurative language to describe the experience. In "The Day Is Done," night is compared to a bird flying in the sky. Darkness falls from the night as a feather falls from an eagle. In "I'll Tell You How the Sun Rose," a clergyman in gray is compared to the gray of dusk. Both poems suggest the gentle, slow qualities of nightfall through their images.

BUILDING VOCABULARY

The Day Is Done   Text Page 319

1. Martial law is law administered by a military authority, either imposed on an occupied territory or invoked by a government over its domain when civilian law enforcement agencies cannot maintain order. A governor might declare a state of martial law to put an end to violent demonstrations or riots, or to secure an area hit by disaster, such as a hurricane, tornado, or major fire.

2. a

3. Karate, jujitsu, tae kwon do, judo, kung fu, aikido

4. Answers will vary. Students may suggest the smell of newly mown grass, flowers, fresh bakery goods, the sea, cologne or perfume, burning leaves in the fall, or even automobile emissions.

5. Answers will vary.

6. Answers will vary; correct responses include *try, attempt, effort.*

7. Answers will vary.

8. Answers will vary; correct responses include *empty, void, lacking.*

9. Answers will vary. Students may suggest that animal life would also disappear and that the entire atmosphere and ecology of earth would change.

10. *Infest* refers to swarming or spreading over a thing or area, or to parasitic attack. *Infect* means to contaminate or spread into a thing or area. *Infest* implies being overrun, covered, or seized by a large number; *infect* implies being invaded, penetrated, or corrupted by a substance, germ, or idea.

11. Students will probably say that they would call an exterminator, spread insect poison, or take some similar action.

12. Answers will vary; correct responses include rats, silverfish, ants, and other vermin.

THE DAY IS DONE *and* I'LL TELL YOU HOW THE SUN ROSE   *(Pages 319–322)*

Henry Wadsworth Longfellow (1807–1882) *and*
Emily Dickinson (1830–1886)

Understanding the Poems

"The Day Is Done" (Pages 319–320)

1. Describe the poem's setting: place, time of day, and weather.

   _____

   _____

   _____

2. In the third stanza, the speaker sets up an analogy: the speaker's sadness and longing is to sorrow as what is to what?

   _____

   _____

3. What does the analogy in stanza three suggest about the degree of the speaker's longing and sadness?

   _____

   _____

   _____

4. What type of poem does the speaker request?

   _____

   _____

5. How will the requested poem help the speaker?

   _____

   _____

continued ☞

"I'll Tell You How the Sun Rose" (Pages 321–322)

6. According to the speaker, which occurs more quickly—sunrise or sunset?

_____

_____

7. To what senses does this poem's imagery appeal? Provide an example for each sense you identify.

_____

_____

_____

_____

Understanding Vocabulary

8. Find *waft(ed)* (line 3), *martial* (line 21), *endeavor* (line 23), *devoid* (line 30), and *infest* (line 42) in "The Day Is Done" and check their meanings in the glossary or a dictionary. Then answer the following questions:

a. Does *wafted* suggest that the feather and the darkness fall quickly or slowly? _____

_____

b. The word *martial* is derived from the Roman god Mars's name. Over what did Mars

rule? _____

c. In your own words, explain what the speaker says the grand old masters' poems and

thoughts suggest (line 23). _____

_____

d. Describe the days and nights of the humbler poet (lines 29–30). _____

_____

_____

e. Does *infest* have positive or negative connotations? _____

_____

continued ☞

Understanding Literary Elements

9. Define a simile.

_____

_____

_____

_____

10. Identify the simile in the first stanza of "The Day Is Done."

_____

_____

_____

11. What two unlike things are compared in the last stanza of "The Day Is Done"? How are they similar?

_____

_____

_____

12. Define a metaphor and explain how it differs from a simile.

_____

_____

_____

_____

13. Explain the metaphor in line 2 of "I'll Tell You How the Sun Rose."

_____

_____

_____

14. Identify a simile in "I'll Tell You How the Sun Rose."

_____

_____

continued ☞

Writing and Responding to Literature

15. Compare the descriptions of nightfall in these two poems.

_____

_____

_____

_____

_____

_____

_____

_____

_____

_____

_____

_____

Building Vocabulary

NAME _____

CLASS _____ DATE _____ SCORE _____

The Day Is Done   *Henry Wadsworth Longfellow*   *(Page 319)*

———————— **IDENTIFYING SYNONYMS / APPLYING DEFINITIONS** ————————

ACTIVITY

In the spaces provided, complete the items below. Use a dictionary to look up any unfamiliar words.

1. Explain what *martial* law is, and tell when a governor might declare a state of *martial*

   law. _____

   _____

   _____

   _____

   _____

2. Write the letter of the phrase that describes *martial* music. _____

   a. a march   **b.** a jazz concert   **c.** an opera   **d.** a classical symphony   **e.** a popular song

3. Give an example of a *martial* art. _____

   _____

4. Name three smells that might *waft* through an open window. _____

   _____

5. What sounds are *wafted* to you from outside your classroom? _____

   _____

6. Write a synonym for the noun *endeavor*. _____

7. Describe one of your *endeavors* during this school year. Tell what you tried to do and

   whether or not you accomplished your goal. _____

   _____

   _____

continued ☞

8. Write a synonym for *devoid*. _____

9. Suppose that the earth were *devoid* of all plant life. Give one result of this condition.

_____

_____

10. Explain how *infest* and *infect* differ in meaning. _____

_____

_____

11. If your apartment were *infested* with cockroaches, what would you do? _____

_____

_____

12. Name three other creatures that might *infest* a home or farm. _____

_____

TEACHER'S NOTES

IT BIDS PRETTY FAIR	*Robert Frost*	Text Page 323
MOON TIGER	*Denise Levertov*	Text Page 324
SILVER	*Walter de la Mare*	Text Page 326

OBJECTIVES The aims of this lesson are for the student:

- To demonstrate understanding of the meaning of the metaphor that Frost uses
- To suggest meanings for the actors, their fighting, and the play's infinite run
- To analyze the poem's irony
- To draw inferences from the poem's metaphor about the poet's attitude
- To identify the central metaphor of the poem
- To draw inferences from the poem about the poet's attitude toward the moon
- To identify details and phrases that convey theme in "Moon Tiger"
- To differentiate between directly stated and implied metaphor
- To analyze metaphors to determine the suggested objects of comparisons
- To express an understanding of how the moonlight spoken of in "Silver" transforms the things it falls upon
- To identify phrases and words that add to poetic mood
- To analyze the use and the repetition of the title word, "silver," in the poem
- To demonstrate a knowledge of how the repeated sounds evoke a sense of stillness and quiet
- To identify words and phrases that suggest the moon's "humanness"

READING/CRITICAL THINKING STRATEGIES

Finding Sequence

Before students begin reading "Moon Tiger," you might ask them to recall childhood fears of monsters under the bed, of the strange shapes that shadows can take on at night, and so on. Tell students that as they read they should consider what the speaker actually sees and what she imagines. As students read, they might draw a picture or a map of the scene. After students have finished their reading, ask them to share their work and to discuss their reactions to the poem.

ANSWER KEYS

STUDY GUIDE

1. It would be almost forever, a very long time.
2. The speaker compares the sun to the lighting for a play.
3. *Pretty* in the title and *if* in line 4 both suggest some uncertainty on the speaker's part.
4. The setting is a bedroom lit by bright moonlight.
5. Creating so many images from the moonlight, the poem's speaker is highly imaginative, and perhaps overly imaginative: The speaker becomes frightened by the imaginary moon tiger. The speaker and the companion (the "you" of the poem) may be children, sharing a room with two small beds and frightening themselves with scary stories.
6. The slats in the jalousies create the stripes.
7. Answers may vary. The air may be cooler because it is night air. The color of the light may look cooler.

continued ☞

8. The objects described in the poem are not really silver. They appear silver in the moonlight.

9. Students' answers will vary but may include *shiny, bright, precious.*

10. The moon and the harvest mouse are the only things that move.

11. *Slowly, silently, silver* (9 times), *shoon, she, sees, silvery, sleeps, shadowy, sleep, scampering, stream*

12. An implied metaphor is a metaphor that is suggested, not directly stated.

13. It is an implied metaphor. Although the word *moon* is used as an adjective to describe tiger, the moon is never directly compared to a tiger.

14. Personification is a figure of speech that gives human qualities to nonhuman things.

15. The moon is a woman who wears shoes, is silent, and peers over all.

16. Both speakers see beauty in the moonlight. In "Moon Tiger," the speaker uses words such as *sleek, silver,* and *smooth* that have connotations of beauty and grace to describe the moon tiger. The speaker of "Silver" repeats *silver* nine times in his poem to highlight the moon's beauty. Although both speakers see beauty, their reactions are very different. The moonlight beauty of "Moon Tiger" is a terrifying one suggested by the poem's central image. The tiger is a beautiful but dangerous animal. The moonlight "prowls" in the poem and frightens the speaker. In contrast, the moonlight of "Silver" creates a peaceful, almost magical scene. The speaker's observations reflect tranquility.

Study Guide

IT BIDS PRETTY FAIR, MOON TIGER, and SILVER (Pages 323–326)

Robert Frost (1874–1963), **Denise Levertov** (1923–), *and* **Walter de la Mare** (1873–1956)

Understanding the Poems

"It Bids Pretty Fair" (Page 323)

1. How long is an "almost infinite run"?

_____

_____

2. To what does the speaker compare the sun?

_____

_____

3. What words in the poem suggest the speaker's uncertainty?

_____

_____

"Moon Tiger" (Page 324)

4. Describe the poem's setting.

_____

_____

5. Describe the poem's speaker.

_____

_____

_____

_____

continued ☞

6. What creates the tiger's stripes?

_____

_____

7. Why does the poet say the tiger's nose is cold?

_____

_____

"Silver" *(Page 326)*

8. Are the objects described in the poem really silver? Explain your answer.

_____

_____

9. What words do you associate with *silver*? List any that you feel are appropriate to the poem's context.

_____

_____

10. What things move in the poem?

_____

_____

11. List the words in the poem that begin with *s*.

_____

_____

_____

Understanding Literary Elements

12. What is an implied metaphor?

_____

_____

continued ☞

13. Is the moon tiger of Levertov's poem an implied or stated metaphor?

_____

_____

_____

14. What is personification?

_____

_____

15. How is the moon of "Silver" personified? What kind of person is it?

_____

_____

Writing and Responding to Literature

16. Describe the speakers' feelings about the moonlight in "Moon Tiger" and in "Silver." Are the speakers' feelings similar or different? Use details from the poems to support your observations.

_____

_____

_____

_____

_____

_____

_____

_____

_____

_____

TEACHER'S NOTES

A SONG OF THE MOON	*Claude McKay*	Text Page 328
MENDING WALL	*Robert Frost*	Text Page 329

OBJECTIVES The aims of this lesson are for the student:
- To identify the aspects of urban life that "A Song of the Moon" emphasizes
- To demonstrate an understanding of this poem's definition of "magic" and explain the lack of this magic in the urban setting
- To demonstrate recognition of the places where the presence of moonlight is magic and where it is not
- To explain why urban moonlight is incongruous, strange, and lacking in magic
- To infer the poet's meaning in addressing the moon as "sad"
- To draw inferences from the poem about the poet's feelings about moonlight's beauty and the proper place for this beauty
- To complete an audience prewriting chart for a description
- To differentiate between the speaker's and the neighbor's feelings about the wall and infer what these attitudes reveal about the two persons in "Mending Wall"
- To analyze the visual imagery of "Mending Wall" as the conveyor of the poem's theme
- To draw inferences from the similes, visual imagery, and dialogue associated with the neighbor about the neighbor's personality
- To attribute character traits to the speakers of "Mending Wall" and explain the attribution
- To suggest interpretation of the symbols "wall" and the "something . . . that doesn't love a wall"

READING/CRITICAL THINKING STRATEGIES

Analyzing the Use of Language
Before students begin to read "A Song of the Moon," ask them to make a list of words or phrases that they would use to create an atmosphere of peace and tranquility. What words or phrases might create an atmosphere of enthusiasm and joy? Tell students that as they read this poem they should determine the overall mood of the poem and identify the words and phrases that contribute to that mood. After students have finished their reading, ask them to compare their findings and to discuss their reactions to the poem. Which of the poems about the moon (McKay's, Levertov's, or de la Mare's) do they prefer?

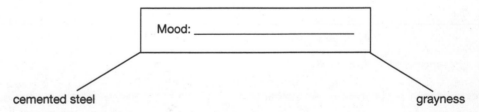

VOCABULARY ACTIVITY **A Song of the Moon**
Solving analogies helps students build vocabulary skills by providing practice with categorizing, interpreting context clues, differentiating between shades of meaning, and examining relationships between words and concepts. To help students master unfamiliar words in "A Song of the Moon," present the following incomplete analogies to the class and have students fill in each blank with an appropriate word. If you have identified other words that have given students difficulty, you may wish to create analogies for those words and add them to the list.

continued ☞

1. amusing : humorous :: lugubrious : _____

2. benefit : hindrance :: monotone : _____

3. sedan : automobile :: tenement : _____

4. unusual : common :: incongruous : _____

5. streams : creeks :: draughts : _____

Answers [Note: These are possible answers; student answers will likely vary.]

1. mournful. *Amusing* and *humorous* are synonyms, as are *lugubrious* and *mournful*.
2. variety. *Benefit* and *hindrance* have opposite meanings, as do *monotone* and *variety*.
3. building. A *sedan* is a kind of automobile; a *tenement* is a kind of building.
4. suitable. *Unusual* and *common* are antonyms, as are *incongruous* and *suitable*.
5. drinks. *Streams* and *creeks* are the same, as are *draughts* and *drinks*.

   With students who are unfamiliar with analogies or who have less-advanced verbal skills, you may wish to write the analogies on the chalkboard and solve them as a class activity. In advanced classes, you can give students handouts or read the analogies aloud and have students copy them.

   When you review answers to analogies, be flexible. Students will likely have a variety of solutions, a number of which may be correct. Some students may even discover relationships between the words, and hence have answers that you had not considered. Be prepared to give credit to any student who can logically support his or her solution. Note: If you have not presented analogies to your class before, guide students in solving the following sample analogies before assigning analogy problems.

   hot : cold :: gigantic : tiny

   strong : powerful :: smart : intelligent

   hammer : carpenter :: pencil : accountant

First, read the analogy; for example, *hot* is to *cold* as *gigantic* is to *tiny*. Then explain the relationship between the words—hot is the opposite of cold, and gigantic is the opposite of tiny. Review as many analogies as necessary to ensure that students grasp the principles involved in solving analogy problems.

ANSWER KEY

STUDY GUIDE

1. The speaker describes the city as mournful or sad in feeling. The city's color is gray and its textures hard (steel and stone) and unnatural. The city has no variety: A million homes are all the same.

2. Although the moonlight falls on all the apartments, it does not change their appearances and thus is of no consequence to them.

3. The speaker says that the moon's silver seems too old and plain or simple to have an impact upon the city's landscape.

4. The speaker describes the countryside as happy or joyous in feeling. The countryside has variety and color and its textures seem soft (flowers, dew) and natural.

5. "Something" (perhaps nature itself) is the first possibility and the one the speaker seems to believe in. Hunters cause breaks in walls but not the breaks the speaker is now repairing. The speaker even suggests "elves" later in the poem.

6. Each stays on his own side of the wall and picks up and replaces the stones that have fallen.

7. The line is addressed to the boulders. The speaker is indicating that the boulders tend to fall down easily because they are rounded and only balanced without mortar to hold them.

8. He thinks walls are necessary if they have a definite purpose, such as keeping animals from wandering off.

9. He says the wall is not needed because walls are supposed to wall something in and something out, but he and his neighbor don't have animals that need to be confined or separated. They have only trees to separate.

10. Spring makes the speaker feel mischievous, and he decides to challenge his neighbor's assumptions.

11. The speaker sees the neighbor literally in the darkness of the woods, but he also sees him figuratively in the darkness of unenlightenment or primitive ignorance. The neighbor is unable or unwilling to rely on past traditions.

continued ☞

12. The neighbor's only words are "Good fences make good neighbors," which he repeats twice (lines 27 and 45). He has learned this saying from his father.

13. A symbol is a concrete word or image that stands for a complex idea or set of ideas.

14. The neighbor symbolizes a blind and unthinking devotion to tradition or accepted ideas or to "the way things have always been done."

15. Students may cite any of the speaker's humorous remarks, lines 17–19, 25–26, or 36, to show Frost's wit. To illustrate the poem's wisdom, they should paraphrase one of the poem's themes, such as the idea that traditions should not always be accepted or continued without question. Circumstance, imagination, and reason can sometimes dictate a new course.

SELECTION TEST

The Day Is Done	Text Page 319
I'll Tell You How the Sun Rose	Text Page 321
It Bids Pretty Fair	Text Page 323
Moon Tiger	Text Page 324
Silver	Text Page 326
A Song of the Moon	Text Page 328
Mending Wall	Text Page 329

A.
1. c
2. d
3. b
4. b
5. b
6. c
7. a
8. b
9. b
10. c
11. c
12. b

B.
13. a
14. f
15. c
16. b
17. c

Study Guide

A SONG OF THE MOON *and* MENDING WALL *(Pages 328–331)*

Claude McKay *(1890–1948) and* Robert Frost *(1874–1963)*

Understanding the Poems

"A Song of the Moon" (Page 328)

1. Describe the speaker's view of the city in the first stanza. Consider mood or feeling, color, texture, and variety.

   _____

   _____

   _____

   _____

2. In what sense is the moon indifferent to each apartment?

   _____

   _____

   _____

3. How is the speaker critical of the moon's "silver" in the third stanza?

   _____

   _____

   _____

4. Describe the speaker's view of the countryside in the final stanza. Consider mood or feeling, color, texture and variety.

   _____

   _____

   _____

continued ☞

"Mending Wall" *(Pages 329–331)*

5. What possible causes for broken walls does the speaker of this poem suggest?

_____

_____

_____

_____

_____

6. Describe the activity of the speaker and his neighbor in repairing the wall.

_____

_____

_____

7. To whom is line 19 addressed?

_____

_____

_____

8. Does the speaker believe walls are totally unnecessary? Explain your answer.

_____

_____

_____

9. Why does the speaker say this particular wall is not needed?

_____

_____

_____

_____

_____

continued ☞

10. Explain lines 28–29 in your own words.

_____

_____

_____

11. Explain lines 41–42.

_____

_____

_____

_____

12. The two farmers are working and talking together. Identify the neighbor's only spoken words. From whom has he learned this saying?

_____

_____

_____

_____

Understanding Literary Elements

13. Define *symbol*.

_____

_____

14. What do you think the neighbor symbolizes?

_____

_____

_____

_____

continued

Writing and Responding to Literature

15. Frost's biographical notes (page 333) indicate that his poetry is known for its wit and wisdom. Explain how "Mending Wall" shows both of these characteristics. Use specific examples from the poem to support your points.

_____

_____

_____

_____

_____

_____

_____

_____

_____

_____

Selection Test

Figurative Language   *(Page 318)*

AN OPEN-BOOK TEST

A. Understanding Poetry.   Write the letter of the *best* answer to each question.
(5 points each)

1. In "The Day Is Done," the speaker is all of the following *except*
   a. weary
   b. sad
   c. far from home
   d. a poetry lover   1. _____

2. Longfellow's poem contains numerous figures of speech. Which of the following *incorrectly* identifies the figure of speech in a line?
   a. Line 2: metaphor
   b. Line 21: simile
   c. Line 27: simile
   d. Line 40: metaphor   2. _____

3. "I'll Tell You How the Sun Rose" contains several figures of speech. Which of the following *incorrectly* identifies the figure of speech in a line?
   a. Line 2: metaphor
   b. Line 5: simile
   c. Line 14: personification
   d. Line 15: metaphor   3. _____

4. The principal subject in Emily Dickinson's poem is
   a. the day's bright colors
   b. the sun's rising and setting
   c. the happiness of nature in summer
   d. a pretty view from a window   4. _____

5. "Moon Tiger" is a poem about
   a. an unusually bright moon
   b. scary moonlight in a bedroom
   c. a pet cat that looks like a tiger
   d. somebody's frightening dream   5. _____

6. All of the following statements about "Moon Tiger" are correct *except* one. Which one?
   a. The poem contains vivid phrases and details.
   b. The poem is based on one metaphor.
   c. The speaker has very little imagination.
   d. The moon tiger goes everywhere in the room.   6. _____

7. All of the following statements about "It Bids Pretty Fair" are correct *except* one. Which one?
   a. The speaker is completely optimistic.
   b. The subject definitely is not a Broadway play.
   c. The title is ironic.
   d. "Lighting" is a metaphor for sunlight.   7. _____

8. In "Silver," the moon is all of the following *except*
   a. a woman
   b. frightening
   c. an on-looker
   d. mild and harmless   8. _____

continued ☞

9. The prevailing mood of "Silver" is which of the following?
   a. Melancholy
   b. Tranquillity
   c. Suspenseful unease
   d. Drowsy amusement

   9. _____

10. In "A Song of the Moon," the speaker views the city as a
   a. magical place
   b. busy place
   c. poor, gray place
   d. lively place

   10. _____

11. Which of the following phrases correctly identifies the subject of "Mending Wall"?
   a. A specific, single morning of wall repairing
   b. Several similar days of wall mending
   c. Both real and figurative barriers
   d. Relationships between friendly neighbors

   11. _____

12. To the speaker, the saying, "Good fences make good neighbors" is which of the following?
   a. A reasonable, true statement
   b. Much too simplified an assertion
   c. The basis of rural friendships
   d. A totally absurd, ignorant assertion

   12. _____

B. **Comparing Poems.** The following questions ask you to compare the subject matter and poetic techniques of these poems. You may use an answer more than once. (*8 points each*)

   a. "The Day Is Done"
   b. "I'll Tell You How the Sun Rose"
   c. "Moon Tiger"
   d. "It Bids Pretty Fair"
   e. "Silver"
   f. None of these poems

13. In which poem does the speaker ask for assistance?   13. _____

14. Which poem avoids all figures of speech?   14. _____

15. Which poem contains an element of unease and fear?   15. _____

16. Which poem involves personification?   16. _____

17. Which poem relies most heavily on the use of realistic details?   17. _____

THE DESTRUCTION OF SENNACHERIB

	George Gordon, Lord Byron	Text Page 334
JAZZ FANTASIA	*Carl Sandburg*	Text Page 337
ELDORADO	*Edgar Allan Poe*	Text Page 339

OBJECTIVES   The aims of this lesson are for the student:

- To interpret similes from "The Destruction of Sennacherib" in order to understand how they create an image of the Assyrian's power
- To demonstrate understanding of the content of the poem by paraphrasing several stanzas
- To analyze a poem's escalation leading to climax, as is seen in stanzas 3–6 of "The Destruction of Sennacherib"
- To analyze the poem's meter, explaining the connection between a poem's meter and meaning
- To draw inferences from the imagery about the alternate intensity and serenity of jazz in "Jazz Fantasia"
- To analyze and recognize the similarities between the poem's improvisational meter and the narrative's presentation of jazz's wildness
- To identify changes in the poem's rhythm
- To interpret the appropriateness of the poem's title as it relates to the poem's text
- To speculate on the eventual fate of characters in "Eldorado" as indicated by textual clues
- To differentiate between very similar, though distinct, words and images like "shade" and "shadow" in this poem
- To identify pairs of rhyming words, and instances of their recurrence
- To interpret the final stanza of the poem

READING/CRITICAL THINKING STRATEGIES

Summarizing

As a prereading strategy for "The Destruction of Sennacherib," you might ask students to discuss what practice they have had in paraphrasing and summarizing. What do they consider to be the hardest part of the task? What is the easiest? Tell students that as they read this selection they should make notes for a summary of the selection. A chart like the one below might prove useful. After students have finished their reading, ask them to compare notes and to agree upon a three- or four-sentence summary of the poem.

Stanza 1	Sennacherib and his troops descend on the people of Jerusalem like wolves on a flock of sheep.
Stanza 2	

Analyzing

As a prereading strategy for "Jazz Fantasia," encourage students to discuss whether isolated sounds can have meaning. Can they have connotations? What sound would students associate with joy? with fear? What effects can the repetitions of sound have? You may want to direct students' attention to *assonance* and *alliteration* in the **Literary Terms and Techniques** section. Be sure that students understand that these terms refer to the repetition of sounds, not the letters of the alphabet. Tell students that as they read this poem, they should consider how the repetition of sound contributes to the meaning and mood of the poem. Students might benefit from mapping their responses. After

continued ☞

students have finished their reading, ask them to share their findings. How do students react to the repetition in Sandburg's work?

> Drum on your drums, batter on your banjoes,
> sob on the long cool winding saxophones.
> Go to it, O jazzmen.

VOCABULARY ACTIVITY

Jazz Fantasia

In the third stanza of "Jazz Fantasia," Carl Sandburg uses several similes and metaphors to describe sounds in jazz music. Have students identify these figures of speech and guess which instrument makes the sound that is described.

Then ask students to create similes describing sounds in rock or some other kind of music. As each student offers a simile, have the rest of the class guess which instrument is being described. You can extend this exercise by having students create similes for other facets of music, such as particular performers, songs, or types of music, or for other performing arts, such as film, videos, or dance.

Students will likely begin by offering clichés. Encourage originality by prompting the class to explore unique relationships. If you have your students keep a log or journal, you may wish to have them record their similes in it and to add to the list when their activity is repeated in connection with other literature selections.

ANSWER KEYS

STUDY GUIDE

The Destruction of Sennacherib   Text Page 334
Jazz Fantasia   Text Page 337
Eldorado   Text Page 339

1. Sennacherib is compared to a wolf attacking a flock of sheep. The connotations of this comparison suggest that Sennacherib is a fierce, threatening, dangerous beast while the people of Jerusalem are innocent and helpless victims.

2. The Assyrian army is compared to summer leaves in lines 5–6. This suggests the army was fresh and large with many troops. The second comparison, lines 7–8, indicates the destruction of the army. Here, the army is compared to autumn leaves, dead and scattered.

3. The Angel of Death visits the Assyrian camp, breathes in the face of each soldier, and kills him.

4. The surviving Assyrians break their idols when they realize their army has been destroyed by a stronger power.

5. The sounds are appropriate because they sound like the instruments they are describing.

6. The jazz musicians are being addressed.

7. The jazz described in these lines is loud. The images suggest frenzied, primal, uncontrolled feelings.

8. The speaker tells the jazzmen to stop their loud, rough style.

9. The musicians follow the order. The music's images become soft and quiet.

10. Students' opinions may vary. Since the knight is described as gallant and bold, he is probably seeking an ideal.

11. *Shadow* means ghost in this stanza.

12. Formal

13. Rhythm is based upon a pattern of stressed and unstressed syllables.

14. Meter is a regular and pronounced rhythmic pattern.

15. Irregular

16. Students' opinions may vary, but they should use specific examples to illustrate their opinions.

LANGUAGE SKILLS

The Destruction of Sennacherib   Text Page 334

A. 1. like   4. as
   2. as   5. as
   3. like

B. 6.–15. Answers will vary.

BUILDING VOCABULARY

The Destruction of Sennacherib   Text Page 334

1. cohorts   6. waxed
2. host   7. mail
3. sheen   8. fold
4. distorted   9. steeds
5. unsmote   10. withered

For information regarding permissioned material included on this page, see pages i–iv.

HRW material copyrighted under notice appearing earlier in this work.

THE DESTRUCTION OF SENNACHERIB, JAZZ FANTASIA, and ELDORADO *(Pages 334–339)*

George Gordon, Lord Byron (1788–1824), **Carl Sandburg** (1878–1967), *and* **Edgar Allan Poe** (1809–1849)

Understanding the Poems

"The Destruction of Sennacherib" (Pages 334–336)

1. In line 1, to what is the Assyrian king compared? What connotations are suggested by this comparison?

_____

_____

_____

_____

2. Identify and explain the two similes in the second stanza.

_____

_____

_____

_____

3. What does the Angel of Death do?

_____

_____

_____

4. Why are the idols of Baal broken?

_____

_____

_____

continued ☞

"Jazz Fantasia" (Page 337)

5. How are the sounds of the words in lines 1–2 appropriate?

_____

_____

6. Who is being addressed in the poem?

_____

_____

7. In lines 9–11, what feelings do the images reflect?

_____

_____

_____

8. What does the speaker mean when he orders, "Can the rough stuff" (line 12)?

_____

_____

9. What happens immediately after the speaker's order in line 12?

_____

_____

"Eldorado" (Page 339)

10. The headnote indicates that a search for Eldorado may mean a search for gold or a quest for an unattainable ideal. Which do you think the knight of the poem was seeking? Explain your answer.

_____

_____

_____

11. In the third stanza, what does *shadow* mean?

_____

_____

continued ☞

Understanding Literary Elements

12. Is the diction of "The Destruction of Sennacherib" formal or informal?

_____

_____

13. Upon what is rhythm based in English poetry?

_____

_____

14. Define *meter*.

_____

_____

15. Is the rhythm of "Jazz Fantasia" regular or irregular?

_____

_____

Writing and Responding to Literature

16. In the last stanza of "Eldorado," the pilgrim shadow urges the knight to continue boldly on his quest. By doing so, the shadow seems to suggest that one's striving or search for an ideal is just as important as actually achieving it. Do you agree or disagree with this idea? Use an example from your own experience or someone else's to illustrate your opinion.

_____

_____

_____

_____

_____

_____

_____

NAME _____

CLASS _____ DATE _____ SCORE _____

Language Skills

The Destruction of Sennacherib

George Gordon, Lord Byron

(Page 334)

―――――――― **COMPARISONS USING "LIKE" AND "AS"** ――――――――

Comparisons can add vitality and clarity to writing. They give the reader a way to understand an unfamiliar thing or action by referring to a more familiar thing or action. Notice Lord Byron's use of comparison in these lines to clarify the attack on Jerusalem.

> The Assyrian came down like the wolf on the fold,
> And his cohorts were gleaming in purple and gold;
> And the sheen of their spears was like stars on the sea,
> When the blue wave rolls nightly on deep Galilee. *(Page 334, lines 1–4)*

To construct accurate comparisons, you need to understand the distinction between the words *like* and *as*. *Like* is a preposition; in formal English, it is always followed by a noun or a pronoun.

　　EXAMPLES　like the wolf　　　like stars

As, as if, and *as though* are subordinating conjunctions; as such, they are followed by clauses.

　　EXAMPLES　as the wolf descends　　　as though they were stars

ACTIVITY A

Circle the correct form within the brackets for each of the following sentences.

1. Byron says the attacking troops were [like, as] green leaves.

2. He says that the defeated army was scattered [like, as] autumn leaves are.

3. Another image says that the foam of a gasping horse was [like, as] sea spray.

4. The last stanza tells us that the Assyrians' strength melted [like, as] snow melts.

5. The poem suggests that a supernatural event has occurred [like, as] natural changes do.

continued ☞

ACTIVITY B

Complete each of the following comparisons in the space provided. Add a noun and its modifiers after *like*. Add a clause with a subject and verb after *as, as if, as though*.

6. My best friend is like _____

7. My friend treats me as _____

8. Writing an essay is like _____

9. He worked on his essay as if _____

10. My room looks like _____

11. I cleaned my room as though _____

12. She entered the room like _____

13. She entered the room as _____

14. My dog acts like _____

15. My dog acts as if _____

NAME _____

CLASS _____ DATE _____ SCORE _____

The Destruction of Sennacherib *George Gordon, Lord Byron* (Page 334)

———————————— **USING WORDS IN CONTEXT** ————————————

ACTIVITY

From the following list, choose the word that completes the meaning in each sentence. Use a dictionary to look up any unfamiliar words.

fold	cohorts	sheen
waxed	strown	host
distorted	unsmote	withered
heaved	steeds	mail
lances	turf	

1. Jeff usually spends Saturday night with his two _____—his best friends since fifth grade.

2. We were surrounded by the large army; a _____ of well-trained men.

3. When Elaine's hair is freshly washed, it has a beautiful _____ that everyone admires.

4. "That is an outright lie!" the defendant cried. "You have _____ the facts to fit your story!"

5. She tried for ten minutes to swat the fly, but the wily fly remained

   _____.

6. Jeff was so unreliable, his affections _____ and waned like the phases of the moon.

7. To protect divers who work in shark-infested waters, an inventor has created a suit of a

   fine _____, made of flexible, overlapping pieces of metal.

8. The shepherd found the lost lamb and returned it to the _____.

9. In Greek mythology, the sun god's chariot is drawn across the sky each day by a pair of

   fiery _____.

10. The plant's _____ leaves indicated that it would soon die.

NEXT! *Ogden Nash*   Text Page 340

THE SHELL *James Stephens*   Text Page 342

OBJECTIVES   The aims of this lesson are for the student:

- To interpret the use of rhymes to create a comic effect in "Next!"
- To analyze subtle relations of a poem's title to its text
- To find in the poem examples of ideas and images that contribute to the comic effect
- To find lines that support the interpretation of the poem as a dream
- To identify instances of end rhyme and internal rhyme in order to differentiate between the two
- To analyze rhyme scheme
- To identify the scene and the sounds of the scene the speaker is imagining
- To analyze changes in poetic mood, like the change in lines 29 and 30 of "The Shell"
- To demonstrate a knowledge of the way poetic music reflects the sound of the poem's subject—the sea in "The Shell"
- To identify instances of onomatopoeia, assonance, and alliteration
- To analyze instances of onomatopoeia, assonance, and alliteration in order to recognize these instances' conveyance of theme

READING/CRITICAL THINKING STRATEGIES

Analyzing

Before students begin reading "The Shell," you might ask them to remember an experience in which they were lost in their imaginations and emotions and were suddenly jolted back to a reality that was quite different from the world of their imaginations—from serenity to turbulence, from the magical to the ordinary, and so on. You might have students list some words or phrases that suggest the contrast. Students might find using a graphic organizer like the one below helpful. Tell students that as they read this poem they should consider the mood that is established as the speaker listens to the shell and lets his imagination take him away. What words and phrases help establish that mood? After students have finished their reading, ask them to compare their findings and to discuss the last two lines of the poem. Why do they think the speaker chose the word *sweet* to describe his reaction to the sound of the cart?

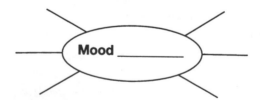

Mood _____

VOCABULARY   **Next!**
Elixir(s) (line 11) is defined in the glossary.

continued ☞

For information regarding permissioned material included on this page, see pages i–iv.

HRW material copyrighted under notice appearing earlier in this work.

ANSWER KEYS

STUDY GUIDE

Next!   Text Page 340
The Shell   Text Page 342

1. The poem is set in the Natural History Museum at night. It may also be set in the speaker's dream or imagination.
2. The skeleton's dancing is compared to a concrete mixer. Both are slow, lumbering, and noisy. A mixer makes a scraping sound, and the skeletons' bones would also scrape.
3. The bones of the skeletons create the music.
4. Examples will vary but might include such occasions as auditions or waiting in line at a deli or restaurant. "Next" is a shortened form meaning "Your turn is next" or "Whose turn is next?"
5. Students' examples will vary.
6. The seaweeds are compared to a creature with long, cold, gray tentacles. The comparison creates an ominous feeling.
7. The poem's mood or feeling is one of loneliness and dreariness.
8. The speaker suggests that the fossils must have drunk some magic potion that restored them to life.
9. Rhyme is the correspondence of sounds in words or phrases that appear close to each other in a poem.
10. End rhymes
11. Internal rhymes
12. *see/be* (lines 1–2) (Students' examples will vary.)
13. Onomatopoeia is a poetic technique in which the sound of the word imitates a natural sound.
14. Students may mention *whipped* (line 7), *hush* (line 16), *rolling* (lines 17–18), *bubbling* (line 19), *swish* (line 20), *croon* (line 26), *whimpers* (line 27), and *jolting* (line 30).
15. Alliteration involves repetition of consonant sounds, usually at the beginning of words close to one another.
16. Students may cite *listened/like/low* (lines 3–5), *slow/sad/seas* (line 6), *winds/waves/waters* (lines 15–16), or *rolling/round/rolling* (lines 17–18).

17. Assonance is associated with the repetition of vowel sounds.
18. The speaker has felt that the place he has heard is lonely and empty of human companionship, so hearing the cart reminds him that he actually has human companionship.
Students' examples will vary but might include being alone in a house and being glad to hear the motor of a car or a key in a door lock.

LANGUAGE SKILLS

The Shell   Text Page 342

A. 1. of the distant seas
   2.–3. of waters, of pebbles rolling round
   4. of slimy gray
   5. of the dreary wind

B. Answers will vary. Following are sample answers:
   6. a beach
   7. distant seas
   8. the beach
   9. light
   10. hear street noises

C. Answers will vary.

BUILDING VOCABULARY

Next!   Text Page 340

1. tread
2. elixir
3. extinct
4. saxophone
5. fossil
6. mammoth
7. mazurka
8. reptile
9. mausoleum
10. dinosaurs

NAME _____

CLASS _____ DATE _____ SCORE _____

NEXT! *and* THE SHELL   *(Pages 340–342)*

Ogden Nash *(1902–1971) and* James Stephens *(1882–1950)*

Understanding the Poems

"Next!" (Page 340)

1. Identify the poem's setting.

   _____

   _____

   _____

2. Identify and explain the figure of speech in line 12.

   _____

   _____

   _____

3. What creates the music at the ball?

   _____

   _____

4. Identify an occasion at which you might hear "Next!" What does this term mean?

   _____

   _____

   _____

"The Shell" (Page 342)

5. To what senses does the poem's imagery appeal? Give an example for each sense you identify.

   _____

   _____

continued ☞

6. Identify and explain the metaphor in lines 19–21.

_____

_____

_____

7. Describe the mood or feeling created in lines 1–28 of the poem.

_____

_____

Understanding Vocabulary

8. Find *elixir(s)* in line 11 of "Next!" and check its meaning in the glossary or a dictionary. How does the speaker use this word to explain the events he witnesses?

_____

_____

_____

Understanding Literary Elements

9. Define *rhyme*.

_____

_____

10. What are rhymes occurring on the final syllables called?

_____

11. When rhyme occurs within a line of poetry, what is it called?

_____

12. Give an example of end rhyme in "Next!"

_____

13. Define *onomatopoeia*.

_____

_____

14. Identify two examples, other than the one in line 6, of onomatopoeia in "The Shell."

_____

_____

_____

15. Identify the specific type of sound repetition involved in alliteration.

_____

_____

_____

16. Identify an example of alliteration in "The Shell."

_____

_____

_____

17. Identify the specific sound repetition with which assonance is associated.

_____

_____

Writing and Responding to Literature

18. Explain what happens in lines 29–30 of "The Shell." Why does the speaker say it was good to hear a cart? What has he been feeling, and how has this changed? Can you recall a similar situation from your own experience? Describe it briefly.

_____

_____

_____

_____

_____

_____

NAME _____

CLASS _____ DATE _____ SCORE _____

The Shell   *James Stephens*   *(Page 342)*

———————————————— ADJECTIVE PHRASES ————————————————

Prepositional phrases can function as adjectives, as well as adverbs. Writers often use prepositional phrases to add descriptive details to their writing. As you read the following excerpt, notice how James Stephens uses prepositional phrases to modify nouns.

> It was a sunless strand that never bore
> The footprint of a man,
> Nor felt the weight
> Since time began
> Of any human quality or stir
> Save what the dreary winds and waves incur.   *(Page 342, lines 10–15)*

A **prepositional phrase** is a group of words that begins with a preposition—a word like *of, by, in,* or *to*—and ends with a noun or pronoun. An **adjective prepositional phrase** or **adjective phrase** modifies a noun or a pronoun. As a rule, adjective phrases follow the words they modify as closely as possible.

EXAMPLES   The footprint of a man,   **[Modifies the noun *footprint*]**

. . . the weight . . . Of any human   **[Modifies the noun *weight*]**
quality or stir

ACTIVITY A

Underline all of the adjective phrases in these lines from "The Shell." Lines 16–17 contain two adjective phrases.

1. Came low and clear
   The slow, sad murmur of the distant seas,   *(Page 342, lines 5–6)*

2.–3. And in the hush of waters was the sound
      Of pebbles rolling round,   *(Page 342, lines 16–17)*

4. And bubbling seaweeds as the waters go
   Swish to and fro
   Their long, cold tentacles of slimy gray.   *(Page 342, lines 19–21)*

5. Was twilight only and the frightened croon
   . . . of the dreary wind   *(Page 342, lines 26 and 27)*

continued ☞

ACTIVITY B

In the space provided, complete each sentence with an adjective phrase. Add a noun and any modifiers for it that you wish to include.

6. "The Shell" describes the experience of a person on _____

7. In a shell, the listener hears the sounds of _____

8. As he listens, he pictures a place like _____

9. All he imagines is colorless and without _____

10. He gladly returns to the world to _____

ACTIVITY C

In the space provided, describe a place you know well. Include at least five adjective phrases in your description. Underline each adjective phrase that you include in your description.

_____

_____

_____

_____

_____

_____

_____

_____

NAME _____

CLASS _____ DATE _____ SCORE _____

Next!   *Ogden Nash*   *(Page 340)*

———————————— **COMPLETING A WORD PUZZLE** ————————————

ACTIVITY

To complete the following puzzle, fill in the boxes with the letters of words that appear in the poem "Next!" by Ogden Nash. Below are numbered clues for each corresponding word in the puzzle. When you complete the puzzle correctly, the tinted boxes will spell out a word that is important to the meaning of the poem.

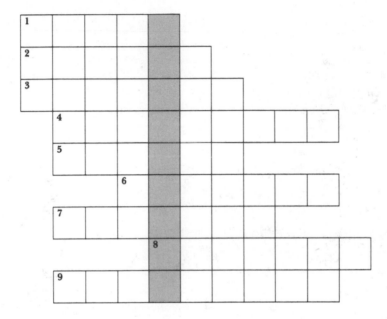

CLUES

1. To walk. You can also do this in water.
2. A mixture of alcohol and something else. During the Middle Ages, some people thought that such a substance would keep them alive forever.
3. No longer in existence on earth. This word describes the dodo and the dinosaur.
4. A musical instrument, a woodwind, often found in jazz bands. This instrument was named after its Belgian inventor A. J. Sax, who lived from 1814–1894.
5. The remains or traces of an animal or plant preserved in rock. This word comes from a Latin word, meaning "dug up." Today, the word is often used to describe fuels made from coal and oil.

6. Huge; enormous. This word is also the name of a prehistoric, elephant-like creature with hairy skin.
7. A lively dance named for the Polish word for a woman living in a region of central Poland.
8. A class of cold-blooded animals whose bodies are covered with scales. Snakes, lizards, and turtles are examples.
9. A building used as a tomb. The word comes from the name of an ancient Greek king.
10. Write the word spelled vertically by the letters in the tinted boxes.

_____

THE KING JAMES BIBLE: PSALM 96
Text Page 345

STARFISH *Lorna Dee Cervantes*
Text Page 347

OBJECTIVES   The aims of this lesson are for the student:
- To examine and interpret thematic and structural similarities in small groups of lines, such as lines 1–3 of "Psalm 96"
- To identify the reasons for and methods of "praising the Lord" as presented by the poem
- To demonstrate a knowledge of the relationship between God and nature as presented by the poem
- To analyze the use of nature imagery to build and intensify poetic mood
- To identify parallelisms and draw inferences from them about the special thematic importance they possess
- To analyze the music devices of Biblical Psalms
- To complete a description chart for a subject
- To infer the poet's intention in associating terrariums with starfish in "Starfish"
- To interpret the use of unusual words, like "shoveled in," (line 15), in order to discover their underlying connotational meanings
- To identify and interpret Cervantes' use of sound devices in "Starfish"
- To complete an observation chart for a subject

VOCABULARY   The following words are defined in the glossary:

Psalm 96				*Starfish*	
salvation	(4)	righteous (ly)	(21)	terrarium (s)	(2)
idol (s)	(9)	righteous (ness)	(28)	pliant	(7)
sanctuary	(12)			flawless	(11)
heathen	(19)			martyr (s)	(13)

VOCABULARY ACTIVITY

Starfish
The following words in Lorna Dee Cervantes' "Starfish" may be unfamiliar to your students:

 jasper
 mussels
 martyrs
 terrariums
 pliant
 artless
 sprigs
 geodesics
 splayed

Choose five of these words, or have each student choose five, and assign all or some of the following exercises for each word. You can review students' responses in class discussion or as a written assignment (either graded or ungraded).

First, ask students to define each word, giving more information than is found in footnotes or in the glossary in the textbook if the word is defined in either place. Suggest to students that they consult at least two dictionaries or other reference sources to obtain this additional information.

continued ☞

Next, have students give five words or phrases that identify what the word is. For example, *quartz* (line 1) is hard, a rock, a crystal used in ham radios, beach sand, and a clear or beautifully colored crystal.

Then ask students to list five words or phrases that identify what the word is not; for example, *quartz* is not living matter, a human product, something to eat, a rare mineral, or a dangerous substance.

Finally, have students write an original sentence for each of the five words chosen.

ANSWER KEYS

STUDY GUIDE

Psalm 96	Text Page 345
Starfish	Text Page 347

1. The psalm addresses the readers.
2. The speaker wants the people to praise the Lord.
3. The psalm offers praise to the Lord and instruction to the people.
4. They refer to a Day of Judgment.
5. The psalm's mood is one of praise and exultation.
6. The speaker is on a beach where thousands of starfish have washed ashore.
7. The speaker views the starfish tenderly, as objects of beauty.
8. The speaker suggests that the starfish might be martyrs, soldiers, or suicides.
9. The speaker is saddened by the deaths of the starfish.
10. The comparison is found in lines 11 and 15. A starfish has five points radiating from a center, and a hand has five fingers radiating from a central point.
11. **a.** *Righteous* (adjective), *righteously* (adverb), *righteousness* (noun)
    b. Lines 5 and 8
    c. *Heathen*
    d. Students' wording will vary: demonstrate the Lord's spiritual rescue.
    e. Students' examples will vary: a church, a temple.
12. **a.** The starfish look like terrariums because their bodies are decorated with objects sometimes found in terrariums.
    b. *Pliant*
    c. She suggests that the starfish might have died for a cause or for their beliefs.
    d. *Perfect* (Answers may vary.)
13. They may be similar in meaning or in structure.
14. Examples are found in lines 1–3, 4–5, and 13–15.
15. Parallelism occurs in the short lists of lines 3–5, 7–9, and 13.

16. *Sprigs/seaweed/seashells*
17. In lines 1–9, the speaker focuses on the beauty of the starfish. In lines 10–15, the speaker tries to make sense of the deaths of the starfish. As she does this, she becomes more objective and detached.

BUILDING VOCABULARY A

Psalm 96	Text Page 345

A. Answers will vary in wording. The following are suggested translations.
1. reign or reigns
2. come or comes
3. you
4. I think
5. You are
6. in truth; really; actually

B. Answers will vary. Sample answers are provided.
7. **a.** A *heathen* is someone who worships many gods or idols and who does not acknowledge the God of the Bible.
   b. *Heathen* comes from the Gothic word *haithno*, and means, literally, "a heath dweller." This is a mistranslation of the word *paganus*, "a countryman," used by Bishop Ulfilas in the fourth century A.D.
8. **a.** *Sanct* is of Latin origin and means "sacred" or "holy."
   b. *sanctuary:* 1. a holy place 2. a place of refuge or safety
   c. *sanctify:* to make holy
   d. *sanctimonious:* pretending to be very holy
9. An *idol* is an image or statue that is worshipped as a god.
10. A *righteous* person would turn it in to a police station.
11. A *self-righteous* person is sure that he or she is morally superior to anyone else. A *righteous* person lives a moral life and doesn't consider himself or herself superior to others.
12. He was interested in bringing souls to *salvation*—to the Christian belief in Jesus Christ.

continued ☞

BUILDING VOCABULARY B

Starfish   Text Page 347

Answers will vary. Sample answers are provided for most items.

1. **a.** *flawless:* without a flaw; perfect. Sentences will vary.
   b. *artless:* simple; natural. Sentences will vary.
2. childless, hopeless, pitiless, merciless, careless, etc.
3. Planets and other heavenly objects
4. Earth
5. **a.** Water
   b. Fish and other water animals
6. *Geologists* study the makeup and behavior of the earth; for example, *a geologist* studies rocks, earthquakes, volcanoes, glaciers, and weather.
7. **a.** "Earth writing"
   b. Maps, countries, cities, natural resources, topography, land features

SELECTION TEST

The Destruction of Sennacherib	Text Page 334
Jazz Fantasia	Text Page 337
Eldorado	Text Page 339
Next!	Text Page 340
The Shell	Text Page 342
Psalm 96	Text Page 345
Starfish	Text Page 347

A.
1. b
2. d
3. a
4. d
5. b
6. a
7. a
8. d
9. b
10. b
11. a
12. d
13. b

B.
14. c
15. b
16. f
17. a
18. d

NAME _____

CLASS _____ DATE _____ SCORE _____

PSALM 96 *and* STARFISH   *(Pages 345–347)*

from **The King James Bible** *and* **Lorna Dee Cervantes** (1954–)

Understanding the Poems

"Psalm 96" (Page 345)

 1. Who is being addressed in the psalm?

 _____

 2. What does the speaker of the psalm want the listeners to do?

 _____

 3. What is the psalm's purpose?

 _____

 4. To what do the psalm's last four lines refer?

 _____

 5. Describe the psalm's mood.

 _____

"Starfish" (Page 347)

 6. Describe the poem's setting.

 _____

 _____

 7. What is the speaker's attitude toward the starfish in lines 1–9?

 _____

 _____

 8. What reasons does the speaker suggest for the deaths of the starfish?

 _____

 _____

9. Describe the speaker's tone.

_____

_____

10. In what lines does the speaker compare the starfish to hands? Explain the similarity.

_____

_____

_____

Understanding Vocabulary

11. Find *salvation* (line 4), *idol(s)* (line 9), *sanctuary* (line 12), *heathen* (line 5), *righteously(ly)* (line 21) and *righteous(ness)* (line 28) in Psalm 96 and check their meanings in the glossary or in a dictionary. Then respond to the following items:

a. Identify the parts of speech for *righteous, righteously,* and *righteousness.* _____

_____

_____

b. Which lines provide context clues for *idols*? _____

_____

c. Which vocabulary word is used to describe those who do not worship the Lord?

_____

_____

d. Paraphrase line 4. _____

_____

_____

e. Name a place that would be considered an example of a sanctuary. _____

_____

_____

continued ☞

12. Find *terrarium(s)* (line 2), *pliant* (line 7), *flawless* (line 11), and *martyr(s)* (line 13) in "Starfish" and check their meanings in the glossary or in a dictionary. Then, respond to the following items:

a. Explain the images created in line 2. _____

_____

_____

b. Which vocabulary word indicates that the starfish have only been dead a short time?

_____

_____

c. When the speaker calls the starfish martyrs, what does she suggest about the cause

of their deaths? _____

_____

_____

d. Give a synonym for *flawless*. _____

_____

13. Phrases or sentences that exhibit parallelism are similar in what way?

_____

_____

14. Give an example of parallelism, other than lines 22–24, in "Psalm 96."

_____

_____

15. Give an example of parallelism in "Starfish."

_____

_____

16. Identify the alliteration in line 3 of "Starfish."

_____

_____

Writing and Responding to Literature

17. "Starfish" reflects two different attitudes toward the same subject. One attitude is expressed in lines 1–9, and another is expressed in lines 10–15. Identify these two attitudes and explain the change.

_____

_____

_____

_____

_____

_____

_____

_____

_____

_____

Building Vocabulary A

NAME _____

CLASS _____ DATE _____ SCORE _____

Psalm 96 *from* The King James Bible *(Page 345)*

————— **ANALYZING ARCHAIC WORDS / ANALYZING AND APPLYING DEFINITIONS** —————

As a language develops, some words drop out of common use and later appear only in literary works and church rituals. Dictionaries usually label such words with the terms *archaic* or *obsolete*, meaning "no longer used." For example, *thee* is an archaic word meaning "you."

ACTIVITY A

For each of the following archaic words or phrases, write the modern English equivalent in the space provided. Use a dictionary if needed.

1. *reigneth* _____

2. *cometh* _____

3. *ye* _____

4. *methinks* _____

5. *thou art* _____

6. *in sooth* _____

ACTIVITY B

Use a dictionary to complete the following items.

7. **a.** What is a *heathen*? _____

   b. The **etymology** of a word is its history, or the tracing of its development back to its origin. For example, the word *cosmopolitan* comes from the two Greek roots *kosmos* ("world") and *polis* ("city"). Locate the etymology of *heathen*. Explain how *heathen* is related in origin to *heath*.

   _____

   _____

   _____

8. **a.** The English root *sanct* appears in the words *sanctuary*, *sanctify*, and *sanctimonious*. Give

   the origin and meaning of *sanct*. _____

   _____

continued ☞

Define each of these words:

b. *sanctuary* _____

c. *sanctify* _____

d. *sanctimonious* _____

9. Explain how an *idol* is different from a statue. _____

_____

_____

10. What would a *righteous* person do if he or she found a bag filled with five

one-hundred-dollar bills? _____

_____

_____

11. Explain how a *self-righteous* person is different from a *righteous* person. _____

_____

_____

12. Why do you suppose General Booth named his organization the *Salvation* Army? _____

_____

_____

_____

NAME _____

CLASS _____ DATE _____ SCORE _____

Starfish *Lorna Dee Cervantes* *(Page 347)*

—————— ANALYZING WORD STRUCTURE AND MEANING ——————

A **prefix** is a word part that is added to the beginning of a word or word root to give that word or root a new meaning.

	Prefix	**Word/Root**	**Combined**
EXAMPLES	un-	fair	unfair
	re-	cline	recline

A **suffix** is a word part that is added to the end of a word or a word root to change its meaning.

	Word/Root	**Suffix**	**Combined**
EXAMPLES	employ	-ee	employee
	reg	-al	regal

The **root** of a word is its core part. Many English words have roots originally derived from Greek or Latin. The word *pompous,* for example, comes from the Latin *pompa,* meaning "display" or "procession." The word *phototropic* is a compound of two Greek roots: *photos* ("light") and *tropos* ("responding to a stimulus"); consequently, a plant that is phototropic is one that responds to light.

ACTIVITY

Sometimes you can use your knowledge of prefixes, suffixes, and word roots to determine the meaning of an unfamiliar word. Complete each of the following items without using a dictionary.

1. The suffix *-less* means "without," "that does not," or "that cannot be." Write a definition for each of the following words, and then use each word in a sentence.

    a. *flawless* _____

    SENTENCE _____

    _____

    b. *artless* _____

    SENTENCE _____

    _____

continued ☞

2. Write three more words that contain the suffix *-less*.

_____

3. The suffix *-arium* means a thing or place connected to another. What does a person learn about in a *planetarium*?

_____

4. If the Latin word *terra* means "earth," what is inside the glass tank called a *terrarium*?

_____

5. a. If the Latin word *aqua* means "water," what is inside an *aquarium*?

_____

    b. Name some animals that you might find in an *aquarium*. _____

_____

6. The word root *geo* means "earth." If the root *logy* means "the study or science of," what

does a *geologist* do? _____

_____

7. a. The word root *graph* means "writing." What does *geography* mean literally? _____

_____

    b. Name some things that you study in *geography*. _____

_____

Sound Patterns   *(Page 334)*

AN OPEN-BOOK TEST

A. Understanding Poetry.   Write the letter of the *best* answer to each question.
(*5 points each*)

1. "The Destruction of Sennacherib" is a description of
    a. a strange battle
    b. an act of God
    c. a fatal plague
    d. the first recorded instance of germ warfare   1. _____

2. Byron's poem uses all of the following elements *except*
    a. inversion   **c.** a rapid rhythm
    b. a regular metrical pattern   **d.** informal diction   2. _____

3. In "Jazz Fantasia," many words are clearly used to
    a. imitate the sounds of musical instruments
    b. give the poem an exaggerated excitement
    c. help set the scene, in a New Orleans nightclub
    d. indicate the present-day enthusiasm for jazz   3. _____

4. In the third stanza of "Jazz Fantasia," the poet suggests or states which one
    of the following?
    a. Jazz players are desperate people.
    b. Jazz players are rough-and-ready musicians.
    c. Jazz music is melancholy.
    d. Jazz music is loud and frenzied.   4. _____

5. In "Eldorado," Poe uses all of the following devices *except*
    a. internal rhyme
    b. irregular rhythm
    c. a fixed rhyme scheme
    d. dialogue   5. _____

6. "Eldorado" makes a philosophical point about quests. Which one of the
    following statements *best* expresses that point?
    a. The joy of a quest lies in the search rather than the quest's attainment.
    b. Every life is a carefree quest that ends in a painful failure.
    c. Human beings never attain the goal of their dreams and hopes.
    d. To fulfill one's ambition takes infinite work and resolution.   6. _____

7. The speaker in "Next!" is
    a. someone who falls asleep in the museum
    b. a member of the museum staff
    c. someone who daydreams about the past
    d. one of the fossils   7. _____

continued ☞

8. After one has read "Next!" what does the poem's one-word title suggest?
  a. That every person dies
  b. That life is only one headache after another
  c. That humans have skeletons too
  d. That human beings, too, could become extinct   8. _____

9. In "The Shell," the speaker says that he
  a. only imagined sounds of the sea
  b. heard waves on a beach never visited by human beings
  c. found a magical "sounding" shell on a remote beach
  d. only imagined listening to a magical seashell   9. _____

10. In "The Shell," Stephens uses all of the following *except*
  a. irregular line length   **c.** simile
  b. a fixed rhyme scheme   **d.** metaphor   10. _____

11. What is the most obvious and most notable device utilized in Psalm 96?
  a. Insistent repetition of urgent statements
  b. A fixed metrical pattern
  c. Internal and end rhyme
  d. Uniform line length   11. _____

12. Psalm 96 is composed of all of the following *except*
  a. praise and description
  b. explicit directions for worship
  c. predictions regarding a Day of Judgment
  d. threats and explicit warnings   12. _____

13. In "Starfish," Cervantes compares the starfish to
  a. lights   **c.** seascapes
  b. hands   **d.** fish   13. _____

B. Comparing Poems.   The following questions ask you to compare the content and poetic techniques of these poems. You may use an answer more than once. (*7 points each*)

  a. "The Destruction of Sennacherib"
  b. "Jazz Fantasia"
  c. "Eldorado"
  d. "Next!"
  e. "The Shell"
  f. Psalm 96

14. Which of the poems repeats a word at the end of each stanza?   14. _____

15. Which poem repeatedly uses the device of onomatopoeia?   15. _____

16. In which poem do we find the most exalted mood?   16. _____

17. Which poem uses a swift meter?   17. _____

18. Which poem uses unusual rhymes and unexpected phrases?   18. _____

TEACHER'S NOTES

THE SOUND OF THE SEA

Henry Wadsworth Longfellow
Text Page 350

SONNET 55 *William Shakespeare*
Text Page 352

OBJECTIVES

The aims of this lesson are for the student:

- To identify which of the sea's sounds are described in the beginning of "The Sound of the Sea"
- To demonstrate a knowledge of the literary term *analogy*
- To interpret and explain the analogy found in lines 9–14 of Longfellow's poem
- To identify the structural features of the Petrarchan sonnet
- To analyze the relationship between the speaker's attitude and the sonnet's structure in "The Sound of the Sea"
- To identify the "living record" that the speaker in "Sonnet 55" refers to and explain why he believes it to be superior to stone monuments
- To analyze and describe the nature of the immortality Shakespeare, or any poet, gives his or her subject
- To interpret Shakespeare's use of the word "live" and to differentiate between this and the usual meaning of the word
- To differentiate between the structure of the Shakespearean sonnet and the structure of the Petrarchan sonnet

READING/CRITICAL THINKING STRATEGIES

Comparing/Contrasting

Before students begin reading "The Sound of the Sea," ask them to recall their analyses of and responses to "The Shell." Tell students that they will be reading another poem about the sea that has some elements in common with Stephens' poem. Ask students to note the major similarities and differences between the two poems as they read. Keeping a chart like the one below might prove helpful to students. After students have completed their reading, ask them to discuss their findings. What do they find to be the most striking similarity? the most striking difference?

	The Shell	The Sound of the Sea
Sound Patterns	*s* slow sad seas	*s* sea, sleep, beaches
Images		
Structure		
Theme		

continued ☞

ANSWER KEYS

STUDY GUIDE

The Sound of the Sea   Text Page 350
Sonnet 55   Text Page 352

1. The sea, which has been calm at low tide (thus "asleep"), has a rising tide after midnight and is then active or "awake."

2. The speaker compares the sound of the rising tide to the sounds of (1) a great waterfall and (2) a roaring mountain wind.

3. Human inspiration

4. By comparing inspiration to sea tides, the speaker suggests that inspiration cannot be maintained at a constant level. Rather, there are highs and lows (like the tides) of inspiration.

5. The speaker suggests that inspiration comes from God.

6. The speaker is probably the poet, who awoke to hear the rising tide and to reflect upon his own poetic inspiration.

7. The poem is addressed to someone whom the speaker loves and wishes to honor.

8. This poem is contrasted to stone monuments.

9. The alternatives are to have the subject represented in a sculpture or to have the subject discussed in a poem.

10. The speaker argues that stone crumbles or is destroyed in battles, but poetry lives in people's minds.

11. You will be immortalized and live until Judgment Day in the knowledge and memory of everyone who reads this poem.

12. A Petrarchan sonnet is divided into an octave and a sestet. Its rhyme scheme is *abba/abba/cdecde.*

13. The Shakespearean sonnet uses iambic pentameter and the rhyme scheme is *abab/cdcd/efef/gg.*

14. Both have fourteen lines and use iambic rhythm.

15. The Petrarchan sonnet introduces and expands an argument in the octave and then concludes it in the sestet. In the Shakespearean sonnet, the argument is discussed in the three quatrains and concluded in the couplet.

16. Shakespeare predicts that his sonnet, and thus its subject, will be immortal. Students' opinions may vary, but this poem has survived for over three hundred years, and Shakespeare's popularity shows no signs of waning.

BUILDING VOCABULARY

Sonnet 55   Text Page 352

Wording of definitions will vary. Suggested definitions are provided. Sentences will also vary.

1. *posterity:* future generations
2. *oblivious:* unaware
3. *masonry:* brickwork or stonework
4. *gilded:* gold-covered; covered with a thin layer of gold leaf
5. *besmeared:* smeared
6. *enmity:* hostility; strong hatred
7. *rime:* a poem
8. *broils:* fights

Study Guide

THE SOUND OF THE SEA
and SONNET 55   *(Pages 350–352)*

Henry Wadsworth Longfellow (1807–1882) *and* William Shakespeare (1564–1616)

Understanding the Poems

"The Sound of the Sea" (Page 350)

1. In what sense does the sea awaken at midnight?

_____

_____

_____

2. To what two things does the speaker compare the sound of the rising tide (lines 7–8)?

_____

_____

_____

3. What is the subject of the last six lines of the poem? _____

_____

4. The speaker compares inspiration to an ocean tide (line 11). What does this suggest about how inspiration operates in people?

_____

_____

_____

5. When the speaker labels inspiration as *divine,* what does this suggest about its source?

_____

_____

6. Identify the poem's speaker.

_____

_____

_____

"Sonnet 55" (Page 352)

7. To whom is the poem addressed?

_____

_____

8. To what does the speaker contrast this poem in the first stanza?

_____

_____

9. In the first stanza, explain the two alternatives for immortalizing the subject.

_____

_____

_____

_____

10. How does the speaker argue that one alternative is better?

_____

_____

_____

_____

11. Restate the conclusion in the couplet of the poem in your own words.

_____

_____

_____

continued ☞

Understanding Literary Elements

12. Describe a Petrarchan sonnet.

_____

_____

_____

13. Describe a Shakespearean sonnet.

_____

_____

_____

14. How are the Shakespearean and Petrarchan sonnets alike?

_____

_____

15. How does the progression of the argument differ in the two types of sonnets?

_____

_____

_____

_____

Writing and Responding to Literature

16. Identify Shakespeare's prediction in "Sonnet 55." In your own opinion, has Shakespeare's prediction come true?

_____

_____

_____

_____

_____

Building Vocabulary

NAME _____

CLASS _____ DATE _____ SCORE _____

Sonnet 55 *William Shakespeare* *(Page 352)*

— USING CONTEXT CLUES / USING WORDS IN CONTEXT —

The words that surround a particular word in a sentence or paragraph are called the **context** of that word. In many cases, the context of a word can provide clues about that word's meaning. For example, consider the following sentence in which context clues provide hints about the meaning of the word *nocturnal*.

> Soon after sundown, the nocturnal creatures of the desert begin to stir and venture out of their dens and nests.

In this example, the phrases "Soon after sundown" and "venture out of their dens and nests" indicate that the "nocturnal creatures of the desert" become active after dark. Consequently, these clues reveal that the word *nocturnal* means "active during the nighttime."

ACTIVITY

In each of the following items, use the context clues to help you determine the meaning of the italicized word. Then, without consulting a dictionary or any other source, write a definition for the italicized word, based on the clue or clues. Check your guesses by looking up the italicized words in a dictionary. Finally, use the italicized word correctly in an original sentence.

1. "I leave this album for *posterity*," Grandma said, "so that future generations can see what life was like in the early 1900s."

   MEANING _____

   SENTENCE _____

   _____

2. Jenny sat calmly reading her book, *oblivious* to the thunder and lightning that terrified her brother.

   MEANING _____

   SENTENCE _____

   _____

3. Do you remember the gruesome *masonry* in "The Cask of Amontillado"? The narrator builds a brick wall around his living victim.

   MEANING _____

   SENTENCE _____

   _____

continued ☞

4. This old *gilded* frame still has the glow of real gold.

MEANING _____

SENTENCE _____

_____

5. From ear to ear, the toddler's face was *besmeared* with chocolate.

MEANING _____

SENTENCE _____

_____

6. Romeo and Juliet fell in love despite the *enmity* of their families.

MEANING _____

SENTENCE _____

_____

7. Jack wrote a love poem to Maria, who pronounced it "the most beautiful *rime* she had ever read."

MEANING _____

SENTENCE _____

_____

8. The *broils* of the Capulets and Montagues have violent consequences; both Mercutio and Tybalt were killed in a street fight.

MEANING _____

SENTENCE _____

_____

TEACHER'S NOTES

MANHOLE COVERS   *Karl Shapiro*   Text Page 354

400-METER FREESTYLE   *Maxine Kumin*   Text Page 356

THE TIME WE CLIMBED SNAKE MOUNTAIN

                     Leslie Marmon Silko   Text Page 359

OBJECTIVES   The aims of this lesson are for the student:
- To identify the manhole covers' eventual fate as indicated by the speaker in Shapiro's poem
- To demonstrate a knowledge of the similarities and dissimilarities between the structure of "Manhole Covers" and other formal poetic structures
- To correctly select instances of parallelism and simile from Shapiro's "Manhole Covers"
- To exhibit a knowledge of what is meant by *free verse*, as it is seen in "Manhole Covers"
- To identify the particular usefulness and difficulties of free verse
- To differentiate between stressed and unstressed syllables in Shapiro's poem
- To classify the details in an encyclopedia article
- To draw inferences from the structure of Kumin's poem about the actual movements of the poem's subject
- To demonstrate a knowledge of Kumin's intended meaning of the word "thrift," and to identify examples of this kind of "thrift" in the poem
- To analyze the evocative effects of alliteration and assonance and how they "create" the sensation of swimming in the poem
- To identify passages that capture the "feeling" of swimming in the poem
- To analyze the visual pattern of the poem and explain its contribution to expressing the meaning of the poem
- To compile a list of details for a description
- To interpret and describe visual images created by the positioning of lines and spaces in Silko's poem
- To infer the speaker's attitude toward the snake
- To analyze the implied attitude toward nature conveyed by "The Time We Climbed Snake Mountain"

VOCABULARY   **Manhole Covers**

Indecipherable (line 3) and *electrum* (line 4) are defined in the glossary. In addition to the glossed words, you may also want to note *pocked* (line 6) and *artifact* (line 9).

400-meter Freestyle

The following words are defined in the glossary:

catapult (s)	(356)	cunningly	(356)	extravagance	(356)
compensation	(356)	nurture (s)	(356)	cadent	(357)

VOCABULARY ACTIVITY   **Manhole Covers**

Several words and phrases in Karl Shapiro's "Manhole Covers" provide excellent subjects for in-depth analysis and research by students. Divide the class into cooperative learning groups and assign each group one of the following phrases:

     savage khan
     Mayan calendar stones

continued ☞

old electrum
chased and scored
Gentle Bethlehem
rustproof artifact
iron-old world

Have each group begin analyzing the phrase by defining its key terms—for example, what is a *khan*? What is the denotation of *savage*, and how does this meaning apply to a khan? What kinds of things are "chased and scored," and how is this done? What is an artifact? How does the term *rustproof* apply to an artifact?

Tell the class to continue this analysis by conducting further research on the key words in the phrase. Recommend the use of encyclopedias, textbooks, and other reference sources. For example, advise students to use an atlas to find out where Bethlehem is; then suggest that they look in an encyclopedia to discover when Bethlehem, Pennsylvania, was founded, and what its history is. Recommend that students look in science and history books to find out more about the Mayans and their calendar stones.

Finally, have each group pull together its findings into a short report giving the meaning and history of the words in the phrase and analyzing the denotative and connotative meanings created by these words. Have the report conclude with a discussion of why Shapiro chose to use this particular phrase in "Manhole Covers."

To allow the whole class to benefit from this research, have each group give an oral report on their findings. To check the completeness, accuracy, and range of each group's work, you will probably want to require a written report also.

ANSWER KEYS

STUDY GUIDE A

Manhole Covers   **Text Page 354**

1. The manhole covers are compared to medals struck by the khan and to Mayan calendar stones.
2. These items are associated with ancient civilizations in Asia and Central America.
3. All are round, large, and made for specific purposes.
4. Both companies make steel.
5. The speaker calls the manhole cover a rustproof artifact.
6. The speaker predicts that our streets will be destroyed and our current civilization will not exist, but the manhole covers will survive.
7. The edges might have notches in them so the covers can be pried up. Thus, they would appear bitten. Raised letters and designs or small holes on the surface of the manhole covers make them seem uneven or pocked.
8. **a.** The Mayan civilization is an ancient one. The calendar stones may be indecipherable because time has blurred or obscured the markings or because the Mayan language cannot be translated easily.
   b. Answers will vary but should reflect the value of the material.
9. Free verse has no set or controlling pattern.

10. Free verse uses (1) everyday language and (2) natural speech rhythms. Free verse has (3) different line lengths, (4) no fixed rhythm, and (5) no rhyme pattern.
11. Shapiro uses repetition (parallelism) and simile in lines 2–5. He describes his subject in the first eight lines and discusses its significance in the last six. This format for discussion follows that of a Petrarchan sonnet.
12. Students' answers will vary, but they might have future generations attach a mysterious or exotic quality to the manhole cover, much as we do now to ancient artifacts.

STUDY GUIDE B

400-meter Freestyle   **Text Page 356**
The Time We Climbed
**   Snake Mountain**   **Text Page 359**

1. The speaker is a spectator at a swim meet.
2. It is the calm surface of the pool's water.
3. The feet rise up quickly out of the water as the swimmer turns for the next lap, and then the feet slide back into the water. This motion reminds the speaker of a hand going up quickly and then back down in a salute.
4. The spectators are watching the swimmer for signs of fatigue.

continued 🔊

5. No, there are no outward signs of fatigue. The swimmer's stroke, kick, and breathing remain steady. However, inwardly, his heart reflects his exertion.

6. According to the poem's form, he does eight laps.

7. The speaker is one of the mountain climbers. Because she cautions her listeners (fellow climbers) about the snake, she may be the leader of the climb or at least someone familiar with the terrain.

8. The speaker cautions her listeners (fellow climbers) to watch for the yellow spotted snake.

9. The snake would be dangerous if bothered. Also, since the mountain belongs to the snake, the climbers should respect the snake's territory and rights.

10. **a.** The swimmer dives with a force that launches him far out into the water, away from the side of the pool.

   b. The swimmer's strokes are skillful. It seems as if the swimmer's strokes displace the water and thus cleverly enable him to move ahead.

   c. Through training, the swimmer has eliminated any wasteful movement.

   d. Speed

   e. *Tick* suggests a regular beat like that of a clock.

   f. The line describes the swimmer's breathing.

11. Answers will vary. Examples can be found in lines 1 and 7.

12. Answers will vary. Examples can be found in lines 3 and 15.

13. In "400-meter Freestyle," the poem's form resembles the swimmer's movement during the eight laps of the race. The lines are exactly even, and the turns are represented by only three letters, always either a three-letter word or the first syllable of a word. These represent the swimmer's quick execution of his turns: flip, convert,

gone. In "The Time We Climbed Snake Mountain," the poem's form resembles a switchback trail on a mountain. A switchback trail zigzags and crosses back upon itself at higher elevations much as the lines appear to do.

BUILDING VOCABULARY

Manhole Covers	Text Page 354
400-meter Freestyle	Text Page 356

1. compensation
2. indecipherable
3. catapults
4. artifact
5. pocked
6. Electrum
7. cadent
8. nurture
9. schooled
10. extravagance

SELECTION TEST

The Sound of the Sea	Text Page 350
Sonnet 55	Text Page 352
Manhole Covers	Text Page 354
400-meter Freestyle	Text Page 356
The Time We Climbed Snake Mountain	Text Page 359

A.
1. b
2. c
3. d
4. c
5. b
6. a
7. b
8. a

B.
9. b
10. a
11. f
12. d

NAME _____

CLASS _____ DATE _____ SCORE _____

MANHOLE COVERS   *(Page 354)*

Karl Shapiro (1913–   )

Understanding the Poem

1. To what does the speaker compare the manhole covers in lines 2 and 3?

   _____

   _____

2. With what time and what parts of the world are the items in lines 2 and 3 associated?

   _____

   _____

3. How are the manhole covers like the items to which they are compared in lines 2 and 3?

   _____

   _____

4. What product do the Bethlehem and United States companies make?

   _____

   _____

5. What is the rustproof artifact to which the speaker refers in line 9?

   _____

   _____

6. What predictions about the future does the speaker make in the last six lines of the poem?

   _____

   _____

   _____

   _____

continued ☞

7. Why does the speaker describe the manhole covers as "bitten at the edges" and "pocked"?

_____

_____

_____

_____

Understanding Vocabulary

8. Find *indecipherable* (line 3) and *electrum* (line 4) in the poem and check their meanings in the glossary or in a dictionary. Then respond to the following items:

a. Explain why the Mayan calendar stones might be indecipherable. _____

_____

_____

_____

_____

b. What kind of objects might be made of electrum? _____

_____

_____

Understanding Literary Elements

9. Identify the pattern of free verse.

_____

_____

10. List the characteristics of free verse.

_____

_____

_____

continued ☞

11. Without many of the familiar controlling patterns of poetry, how does Shapiro achieve structure in his poem? Consider repetition, figures of speech, and the way that the poet organizes the discussion of his subject.

_____

_____

_____

_____

_____

Writing and Responding to Literature

12. Imagine that people five thousand years in the future have found a manhole cover. What might their reaction be? What might they think?

_____

_____

_____

_____

_____

_____

_____

_____

_____

_____

NAME _____

CLASS _____ DATE _____ SCORE _____

400-METER FREESTYLE *and* THE TIME WE CLIMBED SNAKE MOUNTAIN *(Pages 356–359)*

Maxine Kumin (1925–) *and* Leslie Marmon Silko (1942–)

Understanding the Poems

"400-meter Freestyle" (Pages 356–358)

1. Identify the poem's speaker.

_____

_____

2. What is the "perfect glass" that the swimmer catches at?

_____

_____

3. How do the swimmer's feet salute the watchers?

_____

_____

_____

_____

_____

4. When the speaker says, "We watch him for signs," what does she mean?

_____

_____

5. Are there any outward indications that the swimmer is tiring near the end of the race?

_____

_____

continued ☞

6. How many laps of the pool does the swimmer do?

_____

_____

"The Time We Climbed Snake Mountain" (Page 359)

7. Identify the poem's speaker.

_____

_____

_____

_____

8. About what does the speaker caution her listeners?

_____

_____

_____

9. Why does the speaker make this warning?

_____

_____

_____

Understanding Vocabulary

10. Find *catapult(s), cunning(ly), extravagance, compensation, nurture(s),* and *cadent* in "400-meter Freestyle" and check their meanings in the glossary or in a dictionary. Then respond to the following items:

a. Describe the swimmer's dive if he catapults into the water. _____

_____

_____

_____

b. *Cunningly* can mean either *skillfully* or *cleverly.* Explain how both these meanings might be appropriate within the poem's context. _____

_____

_____

c. In your own words, explain the statement "he has schooled out all extravagance."

_____

_____

_____

d. What is the swimmer's compensation for expending his energy and power? _____

_____

e. What word in the same line provides the best context clue for *cadent*? _____

_____

_____

f. What action of the swimmer is described in the line containing the word *nurture*?

_____

_____

_____

Understanding Literary Elements

11. Find two examples of alliteration in "400-meter Freestyle."

_____

_____

12. Find two examples of assonance in "400-meter Freestyle."

_____

_____

Excerpts from this Study Guide are from "400-Meter Freestyle" from *Our Ground Time Here Will Be Brief* by Maxine Kumin. Copyright © 1959 and renewed © 1987 by Maxine Kumin. Reprinted by permission of **Viking Penguin, a division of Penguin Books USA Inc.** Copying only permitted by teachers using the *Adventures in Literature* series.

continued ☞

Writing and Responding to Literature

13. Explain how the forms of "400-meter Freestyle" and "The Time We Climbed Snake Mountain" create visual images that reflect their subjects' movements.

_____

_____

_____

_____

_____

_____

_____

_____

_____

_____

_____

Building Vocabulary

Manhole Covers   *Karl Shapiro*   (Page 354)
400–meter Freestyle   *Maxine Kumin*   (Page 356)

———————————— **USING WORDS IN CONTEXT** ————————————

From the following list of vocabulary words, choose the word that best completes the meaning in each sentence below.

indecipherable	catapults	nurture
electrum	compensation	extravagance
pocked	cunningly	cadent
artifact	schooled	converts
motto	notched	whelked

1. As _____ for her injury, the jury awarded the victim two thousand dollars.

2. The signature on the card is _____, so I have no idea who it's from.

3. Dave is one of those people who _____ himself out of bed at dawn each morning and rushes out the door.

4. According to the museum catalog, this three-thousand-year-old

   _____ is from the time of King David in Jerusalem.

5. The man's face was _____ as a result of his recent battle with smallpox.

6. _____ is a natural alloy of gold and silver.

7. The house was silent except for the _____ beat of the typewriter tapping rhythmically without pause.

8. To _____ your houseplants, give them a sip of liquid fertilizer every three weeks.

9. Walter has carefully _____ himself not to want anything very much for fear he will not get it.

10. Some people feel that a car telephone is a necessity; others believe it is a silly

   _____ .

Selection Toot	

NAME _____

CLASS _____ DATE _____ SCORE _____

Structures   *(Page 350)*

AN OPEN-BOOK TEST

A. Understanding Poetry.   Write the letter of the *best* answer to each question (*10 points each*)

1. In "The Sound of the Sea," the speaker concludes that the sea tides and the inspirations of the soul
   - **a.** awake at midnight
   - **b.** have the same source
   - **c.** are frightening
   - **d.** are omens of disaster   1. _____

2. "The Sound of the Sea" contains or uses all of the following *except*
   - **a.** alliteration
   - **b.** metaphors
   - **c.** stanzas
   - **d.** a formal rhyme scheme   2. _____

3. In Sonnet 55, the speaker asserts the immortality of
   - **a.** the English language
   - **b.** a young woman who recently died
   - **c.** true love
   - **d.** his poem   3. _____

4. Shakespeare refers to his sonnet in all of the following lines *except*
   - **a.** line 3
   - **b.** line 8
   - **c.** line 12
   - **d.** line 14   4. _____

5. In "Manhole Covers," the speaker asserts, or predicts, all of the following *except*
   - **a.** the destruction of city streets
   - **b.** a better storm-sewer system than today's
   - **c.** the end of our present civilization
   - **d.** near immortality for manhole covers   5. _____

6. Shapiro makes use of all of the following *except*
   - **a.** a fixed rhythm
   - **b.** parallelism
   - **c.** simile
   - **d.** metaphor   6. _____

7. The form of "400-meter Freestyle" tells us clearly that this event involves
   - **a.** eight swimmers
   - **b.** eight laps of the pool
   - **c.** a noisy crowd
   - **d.** a champion doing practice laps   7. _____

8. For the speaker in "The Time We Climbed Snake Mountain," the snake
   - **a.** represents nature, and must be respected
   - **b.** represents danger
   - **c.** is beautiful
   - **d.** is a disruption   8. _____

continued ☞

B. Comparing Poems.   The following questions ask you to compare the subject matter and poetic techniques of these poems. An answer may be used more than once. (*5 points each*)

    a. "The Sound of the Sea"
    b. Sonnet 55
    c. "Manhole Covers"
    d. "400-meter Freestyle"
    e. "The Time We Climbed Snake Mountain"
    f. None of these poems

  9. Which of the poems is about the longevity of art?   **9.** _____

10. In which poem is a physical force compared to an abstraction?   **10.** _____

11. Which poem consists of a single sentence?   **11.** _____

12. In which poem is the structure a visual picture?   **12.** _____

TEACHER'S NOTES

AT WOODWARD'S GARDENS	*Robert Frost*	Text Page 362
ART REVIEW	*Kenneth Fearing*	Text Page 364
BRIBE	*Pat Mora*	Text Page 366

OBJECTIVES The aims of this lesson are for the student:
- To identify specific details in Frost's "At Woodward's Gardens"
- To analyze the tone conveyed by selected phrases and words as well as by Frost's poem as a whole
- To describe the poet's attitudes toward the various subjects of his poem, as implied by the poem's tone
- To differentiate between the poet's attitude toward the boy and toward the monkeys
- To analyze the poem's implied attitude toward scientific technology
- To organize notes in logical order
- To identify instances of an ironic and humorous coupling of ordinary objects with lofty descriptive language in "Art Review"
- To interpret the tone created by the various characters' names
- To differentiate between the poet's attitude toward the artists and his attitude toward the world they portray
- To analyze the conveyance of tone by the poem's title
- To differentiate between a word's standard meaning and its meaning as used in a poem, like the word *bribe* in Mora's poem "Bribe"
- To identify the bribes the Indian women and the speaker offer the land and to identify what they are asking for in return
- To interpret and describe the effect of using a word with negative connotations, "bribe," to describe a quite benign activity
- To write a composition analyzing the tone of a selected poem

READING/CRITICAL THINKING STRATEGIES

Drawing Conclusions

As a prereading strategy for "At Woodward's Gardens," you might ask students to discuss their observations of animals, including animal behaviors that seem especially intelligent or particularly odd. You may also want to initiate a discussion of why some people are insensitive to animals. Tell students that as they read this selection they should consider the behavior of the animals and the human in the poem. What does the boy do? Why? What do the monkeys do? Why? After students have finished their reading, ask them to compare their findings and to discuss their reaction to the boy and the monkeys.

VOCABULARY **At Woodward's Gardens**
Solar (line 6), *psychological* (line 19), and *institute(d)* (line 25) are defined in the glossary.

Art Review
Morbid (line 8) is defined in the glossary.

VOCABULARY
ACTIVITY **Bribe**
Point out to the class that the title word in Pat Mora's "Bribe" appears in a different form within the poem, and ask, "What is this form called?" At least some students

continued ☞

should respond that it is a participle. Next ask, "What part of speech is a participle?" Some students will likely answer "verb"; a few may also add that the participle form of a verb can be used as a verbal—a participle or a gerund. Ask students to identify all the participles in the poem, and write each word on the chalkboard as it is given. Then call for volunteers to identify how the word is used in its context—as a verb, an adjective, or a noun. Students should identify "chanting" (twice in line 2); "bribing" (line 3); "kneeling," "digging," and "burying" (line 6); "chanting" (twice in line 8); "singing" (line 10);' "rocking" (line 11); and "yellowing" (line 15) as participles used as adjectives.

Initiate a class discussion on how the use of verb forms as nouns and adjectives affects the tone, rhythm, content, and other features of a poem. Students should recognize that verbs contribute action and liveliness and the *–ing* endings create a sense of ongoing activity.

If you wish, you can extend this discussion by asking students also to identify infinitives within the poem—"to weave" (line 10), "to trap" (line 11), "to smile" and "to croon" (line 16), and "to help" (line 17)—and to analyze how the effect that they have is similar to and different from that of the participles.

ANSWER KEYS

STUDY GUIDE A

At Woodward's Gardens   Text Page 362

1. A boy at the zoo teases two caged monkeys by burning their noses when he focuses the sun's rays through a magnifying glass.
2. The speaker calls it a weapon because that is how the boy uses it: He uses it to hurt the monkeys.
3. Literally, the monkeys are puzzled by this incident in their lives. They don't understand why their noses hurt. On a symbolic level, the monkeys might be troubled or upset that human life (the boy) has not risen above the level of tormenting other creatures.
4. The monkeys snatch the boy's magnifying glass, examine it, and totally destroy it. Finally, the monkeys hide the remains of the glass in their straw.
5. **a.** The magnifying glass collects the sun's rays and concentrates them at a point so that an object held under that point will be burned.
   b. From the speaker's perspective, the incident reveals a truth about human behavior rather than a scientific fact.
   c. *Instituted* suggests a more formal diction and tone. A more informal word choice would have been *set up* or *started*.
6. The speaker's use of words such as *puzzlement, hurt, little,* and *prisoners* conveys a feeling of sympathy for the monkeys. The speaker's choice of details also adds to the sympathetic tone.
7. A moral is found at the end of a fable. In "At Woodward's Gardens," the poem's moral is articulated in its last line. The poem's speaker observes that knowledge in the abstract is not

enough. Humans must learn to use their knowledge correctly and wisely rather than improperly so that the results do not cause misery for others.

STUDY GUIDE B

Art Review   Text Page 364
Bribe   Text Page 366

1. The speaker seems amused by the graffiti.
2. The poem's graffiti is found in public places, some of which are run-down.
3. The speaker uses formal, lofty language in these lines. It sounds like the language of an art critic in a review.
4. The speaker compares the graffiti to marks or bruises on time.
5. The speaker is a writer, probably the poet herself.
6. The Indian women offer turquoise threads, and the speaker offers a pen and paper. Both "bribes" are tools of the women's respective trades or art.
7. They pray to the earth mother for help.
8. The tone is supplicating, prayer-like.
9. Both the Indian women and the speaker ask for help with their work. In both cases, this work is creative and involves translating the beauty of the natural world into an artistic medium.
10. *Morbid* (negative connotations) and *powerful* (positive connotations) suggest a mixed review.
11. The poet uses repetition of either *Know* or *That* at the beginning of each line.

continued ☞

12. Fearing believes that the graffiti artists leave their mark on public places as a way of asserting their individual identity in an all-too-anonymous world. Students may agree or disagree with this **assessment**.

LANGUAGE SKILLS

At Woodward's Gardens   Text Page 362

A. 1. I
     2. P
     3. P
     4. I
     5. P

B. 6. to win, AV
     7. to sew, N
     8. to visit, AJ
     9. To sleep, N
     10. to watch, AJ

C. Paragraphs will vary.

BUILDING VOCABULARY

At Woodward's Gardens   Text Page 362
Art Review   Text Page 364

Answers will vary. Sample answers are given for most items.

1. **a.** To start; to begin something new; to establish
    b. Sentences will vary.
2. Students may name a school, a hospital, a university.
3. **a.** *destitute:* poverty-stricken; lacking the necessities of life
    b. *restitution:* compensation; restoration of losses or damages

4. *Solar* heating uses energy from the sun to heat water, which in turn is used to heat a home.
5. **a.** *solar:* pertaining to the sun
    b. *lunar:* pertaining to the moon
    c. *stellar:* pertaining to the stars
    d. The words all refer to objects in the universe.
6. A *psychologist* gives therapy to people with concerns.
7. Supposedly, a *psychic* has extraordinary spiritual powers to read people's minds, see into the future, and commune with the spirits of dead people
8. A *psychosomatic* illness is one that is caused or aggravated by a person's mind and feelings.

SELECTION VOCABULARY TEST

Dream Deferred   Text Page 306
The Meadow Mouse   Text Page 310
The Farm   Text Page 312
The Day Is Done   Text Page 319
Next!   Text Page 340
Psalm 96   Text Page 345
Manhole Covers   Text Page 354
At Woodward's Gardens   Text Page 362

A. 1. d   4. b
     2. e   5. a
     3. c

B. 1. n   9. c
     2. m   10. f
     3. e   11. k
     4. a   12. i
     5. l   13. d
     6. j   14. p
     7. b   15. g
     8. o

NAME _____

CLASS _____ DATE _____ SCORE _____

AT WOODWARD'S GARDENS   *(Pages 362–363)*

Robert Frost (1874–1963)

Understanding the Poem

1. Briefly describe the poem's setting and action in lines 1–20.

_____

_____

_____

_____

2. Why does the speaker call the glass a weapon in line 7?

_____

_____

_____

3. When the speaker says the monkeys "exchanged troubled glances over life" (line 13), what does he literally mean within the context of the poem's story? What does this phrase suggest on a symbolic level?

_____

_____

_____

_____

4. What happens to the "burning-glass" after line 21?

_____

_____

_____

_____

continued ☞

Understanding Vocabulary

5. Find *solar* (line 6), *psychological* (line 19), and *institute(d)* (line 25) in the poem and check their meanings in the glossary or in a dictionary. Then respond to the following items:

a. Refer to line 6 and explain how the "burning-glass" works. _____

_____

_____

_____

b. Why does the speaker label the incident he describes as a psychological, rather than a

scientific, experiment? _____

_____

_____

c. Does *instituted* suggest a formal or informal diction and tone? _____

_____

_____

_____

Understanding Literary Elements

6. How does the speaker's diction show that he feels sorry for the monkeys?

_____

_____

_____

_____

_____

continued ☞

Writing and Responding to Literature

7. The headnote to this poem compares it to a fable. Where is the moral found in a fable? Where is the moral found in this poem? In your own words, explain the poem's moral, the truth about mankind that the poem's story illustrates.

_____

_____

_____

_____

_____

_____

_____

_____

_____

Study
Guide
B

NAME _____

CLASS _____ DATE _____ SCORE _____

ART REVIEW *and* BRIBE   *(Pages 364–366)*

Kenneth Fearing (1902–1961) *and* Pat Mora (1942–)

Understanding the Poems

"Art Review" (Page 364)

1. Describe the speaker's attitude toward graffiti in the first three lines.

   _____

   _____

2. Where is the poem's graffiti found?

   _____

   _____

3. Describe the speaker's diction in the parenthetical comments, lines 2, 4, and 8.

   _____

   _____

   _____

4. What two items are being compared in line 9?

   _____

   _____

"Bribe" (Page 366)

5. Identify the speaker.

   _____

   _____

   _____

continued ☞

6. Name the "bribes" of the Indian women and the speaker, and explain what they have in common.

_____

_____

_____

7. To whom do the Indian women and the speaker pray?

_____

_____

8. What is the tone of the Indian women's chant?

_____

_____

9. What do the requests of the Indian women and the speaker have in common?

_____

_____

_____

_____

Understanding Vocabulary

10. Find *morbid* in line 8 of "Art Review." Does the chalk portrait described in line 7 receive a positive, negative, or mixed review in line 8?

_____

_____

_____

Understanding Literary Elements

11. Identify one technique that Fearing uses in the second stanza of "Art Review" to unify the poem's structure.

_____

_____

continued ☞

Writing and Responding to Literature

12. Explain what Fearing believes prompts the graffiti artists of "Art Review" to practice their art. Do you agree or disagree with his assessment? Give reasons to support your opinion.

_____

_____

_____

_____

_____

_____

_____

_____

_____

Language Skills

At Woodward's Gardens   *Robert Frost*   *(Page 362)*

——————————————— INFINITIVES ———————————————

Some groups of words can be used as various parts of speech. In this way, writers add variety to their writing. As you read these lines from Frost's poem, think about how each underlined group of words is being used.

> Words are no good: <u>to say</u> it was a lens
> For gathering solar rays would not have helped. *(Page 362, lines 5–6)*

> Came dryly forward to the bars again
> <u>To answer</u> for themselves: Who said it mattered
> What monkeys did or didn't understand? *(Page 363, lines 32–34)*

> It's knowing what <u>to do</u> with things that counts. *(Page 363, line 37)*

Each of the expressions underlined above is an infinitive. An **infinitive** is a verb form that is usually preceded by the word *to*. Infinitives can be used as nouns, adverbs, or adjectives.

EXAMPLES   . . . <u>to say</u> it was a lens/For gathering solar rays would not have helped.   **[Noun, subject of the verb phrase *would have helped*]**

Came dryly forward to the bars again./<u>To answer</u> for themselves . . .   **[Adverb modifying the verb *came*]**

The already known had once more been confirmed/By psychological experiment,/And that were all the finding <u>to announce</u> . . . *(Page 363, lines 18–20)*   **[Adjective modifying the gerund *finding*]**

Be careful not to confuse infinitives with prepositional phrases that begin with the word *to*. An infinitive includes a verb following *to*. A prepositional phrase includes a noun or pronoun following *to*.

EXAMPLES   INFINITIVES   PREPOSITIONAL PHRASES
to answer   to a party
to get   to her

ACTIVITY A

If the underlined group of words in each of the following lines is an infinitive, write **I** in the space provided. If the group of words is a prepositional phrase, write **P** in the space.

_____   1. A boy, presuming on his intellect,
Once showed two little monkeys in a cage
A burning-glass they could not understand
And never could be made <u>to understand</u>. *(Page 362, lines 1–4)*

continued ☞

_____ **2.** . . . it brought
A look of puzzled dimness <u>to their eyes</u>   *(Page 362, lines 9–10)*

_____ **3.** One put a thoughtful hand up <u>to his nose</u>   *(Page 362, line 14)*

_____ **4.** . . . it brought
A look of puzzled dimness to their eyes
That blinking could not seem <u>to blink away.</u>   *(Page 362, lines 9–11)*

_____ **5.** Came dryly forward <u>to the bars</u> again   *(Page 363, line 32)*

ACTIVITY B

Underline the infinitive in each of the following sentences. In the space provided, identify
how the infinitive is used in the sentence. Write **N** if the infinitive is used as a noun; write **ADJ**
if the infinitive is used as an adjective; write **ADV** if it is used as an adverb.

_____ **6.** Anxious to win, the runner jumped the gun at the start of the race.

_____ **7.** Martha wanted to sew her own costume.

_____ **8.** The place to visit for Prairie style architecture is Oak Park, Illinois.

_____ **9.** To sleep with the light on can be difficult.

_____ **10.** He is the runner to watch in the next race.

ACTIVITY C

In the space provided, write a paragraph explaining your plans for the immediate or distant
future. Include at least four infinitives in your explanation. Underline each infinitive that
you include.

_____

_____

_____

_____

_____

_____

Building Vocabulary

At Woodward's Gardens   *Robert Frost*   (Page 362)
Art Review   *Kenneth Fearing*   (Page 364)

────────────── **ANALYZING RELATED WORDS** ──────────────

ACTIVITY

Complete each of the following items, using a dictionary.

1. **a.** The word *institute* is made by adding the Latin prefix *in-*, ("in") to the verb *statuere* ("to cause to stand, to set up, to place"). What does the verb *institute* mean?

   _____

   b. Write a sentence using *institute* as a verb. _____

   _____

2. Name two *institutions* in your community. _____

   _____

3. The following words are related in origin to *institute*. Define each word.

   a. *destitute* [*de-* ("down, away") + *statuere*]

   _____

   b. *restitution* [*re-* ("again") + *statuere*]

   _____

4. *Solar* comes from the Latin word *sol*, which means "sun." Explain what *solar* heating is.

   _____

   _____

   _____

5. Define each of the following words.

   a. *solar* _____

   b. *lunar* _____

continued ☞

c. *stellar* _____

d. What do *solar*, *lunar*, and *stellar* have in common? _____

_____

6. *Psychology* comes from the Greek word *psychē*, which means "soul," and the root *logy*, which means "the science or study of." What does a *psychologist* do? _____

_____

7. If a person is *psychic*, what can he or she supposedly do that ordinary people cannot

do? _____

_____

8. *Psychosomatic* comes from two Greek words: *psychē* and *sōma* ("body"). What is a

psychosomatic illness? _____

_____

Dream Deferred	*Langston Hughes*	(Page 306)
The Meadow Mouse	*Theodore Roethke*	(Page 310)
The Fawn	*Edna St. Vincent Millay*	(Page 312)
The Day is Done	*Henry Wadsworth Longfellow*	(Page 319)
Next!	*Ogden Nash*	(Page 340)
Psalm 96	from *The King James Bible*	(Page 345)
Manhole Covers	*Karl Shapiro*	(Page 354)
At Woodward's Gardens	*Robert Frost*	(Page 362)

———————————— **VOCABULARY TEST** ————————————

A. In the space provided, write the letter of the word taken from the list below which is closest in meaning to the italicized synonym or definition in each of the following sentences. (5 points each)

a. martial	**c.** absurd	**e.** nuzzled
b. wafted	**d.** festers	**f.** psychological

_____ **1.** Langston Hughes wonders if a deferred dream (*develops pus; rots*).

_____ **2.** The meadow mouse (*snuggled*) in the man's hand.

_____ **3.** The meadow mouse had (*ridiculous*) whiskers.

_____ **4.** Longfellow tells of a feather being (*carried gently through the air*) from the sky.

_____ **5.** Longfellow also mentions (*military*) music suggested by the poet's thoughts.

B. Match the words given below with the numbered definitions which follow. Place the letter of each word you choose in the space provided. (5 points each)

a. retrieve	**g.** salvation	**m.** righteousness
b. cleft	**h.** solar	**n.** indecipherable
c. endeavor	**i.** idol	**o.** electrum
d. devoid	**j.** sanctuary	**p.** institute
e. infest	**k.** heathen	
f. elixir	**l.** righteously	

_____ **1.** that cannot be made understandable

_____ **2.** fairness; moral rightness

_____ **3.** to swarm over in a destructive way

_____ **4.** to bring back

_____ **5.** fairly; rightly

continued ☞

_____ **6.** a sacred place

_____ **7.** a gap; an opening

_____ **8.** a light yellow metal, made of gold and silver

_____ **9.** an earnest effort

_____ **10.** a substance that is supposed to extend life indefinitely

_____ **11.** people who worship many gods and idols

_____ **12.** a false god

_____ **13.** without

_____ **14.** to start

_____ **15.** a rescue from danger or evil; redemption

TEACHER'S NOTES

THE CHARGE OF THE LIGHT BRIGADE

Alfred, Lord Tennyson   Text Page 367

THE BATTLE OF BLENHEIM

Robert Southey   Text Page 370

OBJECTIVES   The aims of this lesson are for the student:

- To demonstrate understanding of the soldiers' motivation in charging the guns
- To interpret and explain recurring phrases or lines in poetry, like the line "All the world wondered" in Tennyson's poem
- To explain Tennyson's attitude toward the men in the Light Brigade
- To identify poetic sound devices that help create a "feeling" of battle
- To analyze the use and purpose of repetition in "The Charge of the Light Brigade"
- To infer the poet's attitude toward the events described in the poem
- To identify what Old Kaspar in Southey's poem does remember, and suggest why he does not remember what the battle was fought for
- To demonstrate an understanding of the irony in the repetition of the phrases "great victory" and "famous victor"
- To identify each character's attitude toward the battle, as indicated in the poem's text
- To differentiate between the old man's and the children's attitude toward the battle
- To evaluate the details for an objective or subjective description

READING/CRITICAL THINKING STRATEGIES

Comparing/Contrasting

As a prereading strategy for "The Charge of the Light Brigade" and "The Battle of Blenheim," ask students to discuss the attitudes human beings can have toward war. (It is glorious; it is a necessary evil; it is unnecessary, and so on.) Tell students that these poems they are about to read have something in common—they are both about famous battles— but there is a distinct difference in their tones. Ask that students note other similarities and differences as they read the two poems. Students might benefit from keeping a chart like the one below. After students have finished their reading, ask them to share their findings and to decide which poem they find most effective.

The Charge of the Light Brigade	The Battle of Blenheim
The focus is on the soldiers. The speaker seems to assume that the charge will always be remembered.	The focus is on civilians. The characters don't know what the battle was about.

continued ☞

STUDY GUIDE

The Charge of the Light Brigade Text Page 367
The Battle of Blenheim Text Page 370

1. Lines 11–12
2. The speaker compares death to a monster that opens its jaws to swallow men and then closes its jaws so that the men cannot escape.
3. There were some survivors from the charge of the Light Brigade, but losses were heavy.
4. The poem is set outside a cottage near Blenheim, Germany, on a summer evening. Although we cannot pinpoint a date, references in the poem suggest a time at least fifty to sixty years after the Battle of Blenheim, fought in 1704.
5. Old Kaspar is a German peasant farmer. Wilhelmine and Peterkin are Old Kaspar's grandchildren.
6. The scene is one of peace and quiet and rest.
7. Peterkin finds the skull of a soldier killed during the Battle of Blenheim.
8. Kaspar's reaction is very casual and matter-of-fact, accepting of events. Evidently, finding skulls is a common occurrence for him. His only overt response is a shake of his head and a sigh.
9. Old Kaspar remembers factual details: who fought and who won. The English (and Austrians) fought the French, and the English won.
10. Old Kaspar is not sure why the battle or war was fought.
11. According to Old Kaspar, everybody says it was a great victory. This statement shows Old Kaspar's unquestioning acceptance of common knowledge.
12. Wilhelmine thinks the battle was wicked. Peterkin questions what good the battle did.
13. The speaker sees the soldiers as obedient (lines 13–15). He calls them bold (line 23) and noble (line 55). The soldiers' actions in the face of incredible odds are described as valiant and courageous (lines 27–29). The speaker views these soldiers as heroes (line 44) who should be honored (lines 53–54) for their glorious deeds.

LANGUAGE SKILLS

The Battle of Blenheim Text Page 370

A. 1. <u>She</u> <u>saw</u> her brother Peterkin
Roll something large and round,

Which he beside the rivulet
In playing there had found;
<u>He</u> <u>came</u> to ask what he had found,
2. Old Kaspar <u>took</u> it from the boy,
Who stood expectant by;
And then the old <u>man</u> <u>shook</u> his head,
3. My <u>father</u> <u>lived</u> at Blenheim then,
Yon little stream hard by;
<u>They</u> <u>burnt</u> his dwelling to the ground
4. And many a childing <u>mother</u> then
And newborn <u>baby</u> <u>died</u>;
But <u>things</u> like that, you know, <u>must be</u>
At every famous victory.
5. For many thousand <u>bodies</u> here
<u>Lay</u> rotting in the sun;
But <u>things</u> like that, you know, <u>must be</u>
After a famous victory.

B. 6. Old Kaspar didn't know the details; he only knew it was a famous battle.
7. The boy asks what good the battle did; his grandfather doesn't know.
8. The poem tells us something about human nature; it says we rely on opinion.
9. Wilhelmine, who is Old Kaspar's granddaughter, says the killing was wicked; but her grandfather thinks it was glorious.
10. The present scene is peaceful; and, as an old man sits before his cottage, he talks to his grandchildren.

SELECTION TEST

At Woodward's Gardens	Text Page 362
Art Review	Text Page 364
Bribe	Text Page 366
The Charge of the Light Brigade	Text Page 367
The Battle of Blenheim	Text Page 370

A. 1. d   6. b
2. b   7. a
3. d   8. a
4. b   9. c
5. c   10. c

B. 11. b   14. d
12. c   15. a
13. b, d

Study Guide

For information regarding permissioned material included on this page, see pages ii–iv.

THE CHARGE OF THE LIGHT BRIGADE
and THE BATTLE OF BLENHEIM   *(Pages 367–372)*

Alfred, Lord Tennyson (1809–1892) *and* Robert Southey (1774–1843)

Understanding the Poems

"The Charge of the Light Brigade" (Pages 367–369)

1. What lines indicate that the soldiers knew their orders were in error?

   _____

2. To what is death compared in line 24?

   _____

   _____

   _____

3. What does the speaker suggest in lines 37–38 and 48–49?

   _____

   _____

"The Battle of Blenheim" (Pages 370–372)

4. Describe the poem's setting.

   _____

   _____

   _____

   _____

5. Identify the characters in the poem's story.

   _____

   _____

   _____

HRW material copyrighted under notice appearing earlier in this work.

continued ☞

6. What feeling is suggested by the scene described in the first two stanzas?

_____

_____

7. What discovery of Peterkin's interrupts this scene?

_____

_____

8. What is Old Kaspar's reaction to this discovery?

_____

_____

_____

_____

9. What details about the war does Old Kaspar provide in stanza 6?

_____

_____

_____

10. What detail about the war is Old Kaspar not able to provide in stanza 6?

_____

_____

11. According to Old Kaspar, who says the Battle of Blenheim was a famous victory?

_____

_____

_____

12. What are the children's reactions to their grandfather's description of the battle?

_____

_____

_____

continued ☞

Writing and Responding to Literature

13. Describe the speaker's attitude toward or feelings for the soldiers of the Light Brigade. Refer to specific details in the poem to support your answer.

_____

_____

_____

_____

_____

_____

_____

_____

_____

_____

NAME _____

CLASS _____ DATE _____ SCORE _____

Language Skills

The Battle of Blenheim   *Robert Southey*   *(Page 370)*

———————————— SEMICOLONS ————————————

Writers have many ways to show a relationship between ideas. They may use subordinate clauses, or they may create a compound sentence by connecting two ideas with *and, but, or, nor, for* or *yet.* Writers may also connect closely related ideas presented in separate clauses with punctuation marks. Notice how Robert Southey uses punctuation in the following lines:

> It was a summer evening;
>   Old Kaspar's work was done,
> And he before his cottage door
>   Was sitting in the sun,
>   And by him sported on the green
> His little grandchild Wilhelmine.   *(Page 370, lines 1–6)*

Notice that the first line ends with a **semicolon**. The semicolon separates closely related independent clauses in a sentence if the clauses are <u>not</u> joined by *and, but, or, nor, for* or *yet.* The first stanza of Robert Southey's poem is one sentence, but it contains four independent clauses.

> It was a summer evening;   (1)
>   Old Kaspar's work was done,   (2)
> And he before his cottage door   (3)
>   was sitting in the sun,
>   And by him sported on the green   (4)
> His little grandchild Wilhelmine.   *(lines 1–6)*

In these lines, the first clause sets the general scene for the poem. The next three clauses are closely related to the first. They provide specific details for the general scene. The first clause is joined to the others with a semicolon. Notice that the other three clauses that add specific detail are joined to each other with a comma and the word *and.* A semicolon may be used to separate independent clauses joined by *and, but, or, nor, for,* or *yet* when there are commas within the clauses. Under these circumstances, the semicolon makes the division between the clauses clear.

> EXAMPLE   "I find them in the garden,
>   For there's many here about;
>   And often, when I go to plow,
>   The plowshare turns them out!   *(Page 371, lines 19–22)*

continued ☞

ACTIVITY A

Each of the following groups of lines contains two independent clauses separated by a semicolon. Underline the simple subject of each independent clause once. Underline the simple predicate (the verb) of each independent clause twice.

EXAMPLE   It was a summer evening;
          Old Kaspar's work was done.   *(Page 370, lines 1–2)*

1. She saw her brother Peterkin
      Roll something large and round,
   Which he beside the rivulet
      In playing there had found;
   He came to ask what he had found,   *(Page 370, lines 7–11)*

2. Old Kaspar took it from the boy,
      Who stood expectant by;
   And then the old man shook his head,   *(Page 371, lines 13–15)*

3. "My father lived at Blenheim then,
      Yon little stream hard by;
   They burnt his dwelling to the ground,   *(Page 371, lines 37–39)*

4. And many a childing mother then
      And newborn baby died;
   But things like that, you know, must be
   At every famous victory.   *(Page 371, lines 45–48)*

5. For many thousand bodies here
      Lay rotting in the sun;
   But things like that, you know, must be
   After a famous victory.   *(Page 372, lines 51–54)*

ACTIVITY B

In the space provided, combine each of the following pairs of sentences. Use a semicolon to connect the two independent clauses in items 6–8. Use a semicolon and a coordinating conjunction, such as *and* or *but,* to connect the two clauses in items 9–10.

6. Old Kaspar didn't know the details. [semicolon]
   He only knew it was a famous battle.

_____

_____

continued 🖙

7. The boy asks what good the battle did. [semicolon]
His grandfather doesn't know.

_____

_____

8. The poem tells us something about human nature. [semicolon]
It says we rely on opinion.

_____

_____

9. Wilhelmine, who is Old Kaspar's granddaughter, says the killing was wicked.
[semicolon and coordinating conjunction]
Her grandfather thinks it was glorious.

_____

_____

10. The present scene is peaceful. [semicolon and coordinating conjunction]
As an old man sits before his cottage, he talks to his grandchildren.

_____

_____

Selection Test

Tone   (Page 361)
Poems for Comparison   (Page 367)

AN OPEN-BOOK TEST

A. Understanding Poetry. Write the letter of the *best* answer to each question.
(*7 points each*)

1. A boy is doing what to two monkeys in "At Woodward's Gardens"?
 a. Examining them   **c.** Making friends with them
 b. Teaching them   **d.** Experimenting with them   **1.** _____

2. What does the boy learn from his encounter with the two little monkeys?
 a. Monkeys are not interested in people.
 b. A monkey's hand is quicker than a boy's.
 c. It doesn't pay to take valuable objects to a zoo.
 d. Monkeys like peanuts better than magnifying glasses.   **2.** _____

3. The final two lines of Frost's poem suggest that the speaker believes which
 of the following?
 a. Victims deserve sympathy and the right to strike back.
 b. Nobody can even guess what goes on inside a monkey's head.
 c. Monkeys are greatly underrated as thinking creatures.
 d. Practical knowledge is often more useful than theoretical knowledge.   **3.** _____

4. The first three lines of "Art Review" suggest that the speaker finds graffiti
 a. annoying   **c.** important
 b. amusing   **d.** an improvement over ads   **4.** _____

5. A common feature of the four examples of art "reviewed" in the poem is
 the fact that they are
 a. in full color   **c.** all unsigned
 b. quite large   **d.** critical of society   **5.** _____

6. All of the following statements, based on the first line of stanza 2 of "Art
 Review," are correct *except* one. Which one?
 a. The sober language is modeled after legal phraseology.
 b. Most graffiti can be identified by thumbprints.
 c. The speaker is making a public, general announcement.
 d. The speaker believes graffiti say something about the times.   **6.** _____

7. In "Bribe," what is the tone used by the Indian women?
 a. Supplicating   **c.** Playful
 b. Boastful   **d.** Indifferent   **7.** _____

8. The "turquoise threads" that the women bury come from
 a. the material that they will weave
 b. Indian jewelry
 c. the hems of their own clothing
 d. the desert itself   **8.** _____

continued ☞

9. Lines 13–15 of "The Charge of the Light Brigade" describe
   a. failure of the intellect   **c.** blind obedience
   b. faith in violence   **d.** a desire for self-destruction   **9.** _____

10. In "The Battle of Blenheim," the poet makes the point that
   a. wars create noble heroes
   b. the results of wars are often glorious
   c. wars destroy and their purposes are often not remembered
   d. wars affect only the soldier   **10.** _____

B.   Understanding Poetic Techniques.   Identify the poetic devices and techniques used in the following quoted lines from four of the poems in your textbook. You may use an answer more than once. Note that some questions may require you to supply two answers. (*9 points each*)

   a. Informal diction   **c.** Onomatopoeia
   b. Repetition or parallelism   **d.** Simile or metaphor

11. "They might not understand a burning-glass. They might not understand
   the sun itself."   **11.** _____

12. "I ask the Land . . . to croon softly,"   **12.** _____

13. "Know then by these presents, know all men by these signs
   and omens, by these simple thumbprints on the throat of
   time,"   **13.** _____

14. "They that had fought so well
   Came through the jaws of death,"   **14.** _____

15. "'Now tell us all about the war,
   And what they fought each other for.'"   **15.** _____

TEACHER'S NOTES

JOHN ANDERSON MY JO
Robert Burns   Text Page 375

O MISTRESS MINE
William Shakespeare   Text Page 376

OBJECTIVES   The aims of this lesson are for the student:

- To identify the speaker in "John Anderson My Jo"
- To demonstrate understanding of what the speaker is saying to her jo
- To analyze phrases such as "sleep thegither at the foot" in order to extract their symbolic meaning
- To interpret how sound devices—alliteration and repetition, for instance—contribute to poetic music
- To speculate on the reasons for the wide popularity of "John Anderson My Jo"
- To identify the lines of "O Mistress Mine" in which the speaker pleads for his beloved's love
- To demonstrate an understanding of the argument presented in lines 7–10 of Shakespeare's poem
- To revise a letter to include precise words

VOCABULARY   **O Mistress Mine**
Endure (line 12) is defined in the glossary.

ANSWER KEYS

STUDY GUIDE

John Anderson My Jo   Text Page 375
O Mistress Mine   Text Page 376

1. John Anderson and the speaker are sweethearts. Since they have been together so long, we assume they are married although this is not explicitly stated in the poem.
2. The similes are found in lines 3 and 6. John Anderson's hair has changed from black to white.
3. The relationship seems to be an enduring, happy, and companionable one.
4. The speaker is a young man speaking to his lover.
5. The speaker says that love is not something that gets larger or better by waiting. Rather, love needs to be acted upon when one is young and can still feel love.
6. The listener seems to resist the speaker's love and has apparently told him that she wants to wait, to save love for a later time.
7. The young lover in Shakespeare's poem seems to think that love diminishes as one gets older. But the speaker in Burns's poem would certainly disagree since she has loved well into old age.
8. Youth is something that will not last. (Students' wording may vary.)

9. Lines 1 (*j* sound), 3 (*l* sound), and 4 (*b* sound) provide examples.
10. Students' responses will vary but should include an explanation for their beliefs.

LANGUAGE SKILLS

O Mistress Mine   Text Page 376

A.
1. true-love's, true-love is
2. Youth's, Youth is
3. Feste's, Feste is
4. shouldn't, should not
5. You're, You are

B.
6. isn't
7. Aren't
8. can't
9. shouldn't
10. It's

C.
11. It's, I'll
12. They're
13. library's
14. you're, I'll
15. Who's

D.
16. It's
17. they're
18. who's
19. You're
20. it's

Study Guide

NAME _____

CLASS _____ DATE _____ SCORE _____

JOHN ANDERSON MY JO *and*
O MISTRESS MINE *(Pages 375–376)*

Robert Burns *(1759–1796) and* William Shakespeare *(1564–1616)*

Understanding the Poems

"John Anderson My Jo" (Page 375)

1. Explain the relationship of John Anderson to the speaker.

   _____

   _____

   _____

2. What two similes in the first stanza describe John Anderson's hair? How has it changed?

   _____

   _____

   _____

3. Describe the relationship between John Anderson and the speaker.

   _____

   _____

"O Mistress Mine" (Page 376)

4. Identify the poem's speaker.

   _____

   _____

5. What is the speaker's notion of love?

   _____

   _____

   _____

continued ☞

6. What seems to be the listener's attitude, judging from what the speaker says?

_____

_____

_____

7. Explain how the speakers in Robert Burns's poem and Shakespeare's poem differ in their views of love.

_____

_____

_____

_____

Understanding Vocabulary

8. Find *endure* (line 12) in "O Mistress Mine" and check its meaning in the glossary or in a dictionary. Then paraphrase line 12.

_____

_____

Understanding Literary Elements

9. Find an example of alliteration in "John Anderson My Jo."

_____

_____

Writing and Responding to Literature

10. Do you agree with the speaker in "O Mistress Mine" that love is best when you are young? Or do you think, like the speaker in "John Anderson My Jo," that love can endure and grow more meaningful as you get older? Explain why you believe as you do.

_____

_____

_____

_____

NAME _____

CLASS _____ DATE _____ SCORE _____

O Mistress Mine   *William Shakespeare*   *(Page 376)*

—————— CONTRACTIONS ——————

A **contraction** is a shortened form of a word or group of words. An apostrophe shows where a letter or letters have been omitted in a contraction. As you read the lines from "O Mistress Mine," notice William Shakespeare's use and punctuation of contractions.

> What is love? 'Tis not hereafter;
> Present mirth hath present laughter;
>   What's to come is still unsure: *(Page 376, lines 7–9)*

Most contractions are formed by combining two words, with one or more letters left out.

EXAMPLES   'Tis   It is

What's   What is

ACTIVITY A

Underline the contraction in each of the following lines or sentences. In the blank provided, write the complete expression that has been shortened in the contraction.

EXAMPLE   That's not what I meant.   _____That is_____

_____ **1.** O, stay and hear, your true-love's coming, *(Page 376, line 2)*

_____ **2.** Youth's a stuff will not endure. *(Page 376, line 12)*

_____ **3.** Feste's singing about love.

_____ **4.** The speaker suggests that lovers shouldn't wait.

_____ **5.** The speaker would agree with the saying, "You're only young once."

ACTIVITY B

Insert apostrophes where they are needed in each of the following sentences.

6. This isnt what I studied.

7. Arent you going to be at Mary's party?

8. I cant understand geometry.

continued ☞

9. You shouldnt be mean to your little sister.

10. Its only thirty-six days until my birthday.

ACTIVITY C

In each of the following sentences, change the underlined expressions into contractions. Write the contractions in the spaces provided.

11. It is certain that I will take Latin next year. _____

    _____

12. They are offering a reward for information about the burglary.

    _____

13. The library is closed on Sundays. _____

14. If you are too busy, I will take her to the doctor. _____

    _____

15. Who is candidate for sophomore class president? _____

Be careful not to confuse contractions with possessive pronouns.

CONTRACTIONS	POSSESSIVE PRONOUNS
Who's coming? [Who is]	Whose sweater is it?
It's torn. [It is]	Its cover is torn.
You're sorry. [You are]	Your regret is genuine.
They're leaving. [They are]	Their departure is sudden.
There's still time. [There is]	The car is theirs.

ACTIVITY D

Select the correct word from the choices given within brackets in each of the following sentences. Write your choice in the space provided.

_____ 16. [It's, Its] fun to imagine myself ten years in the future.

_____ 17. This summer, [their, they're] visiting France and Spain.

_____ 18. My mother, [whose, who's] a lawyer, enjoys helping other people.

_____ 19. [You're, Your] on the list of students with high averages.

_____ 20. Whenever [its, it's] hot, my dog jumps in the swimming pool.

TEACHER'S NOTES

I WANDERED LONELY AS A CLOUD
William Wordsworth   Text Page 377

LOVELIEST OF TREES   *A. E. Housman*   Text Page 379

OBJECTIVES

The aims of this lesson are for the student:
- To differentiate between the speaker's mood before and after his encounter with the daffodils
- To analyze the importance of the flowers to the speaker—the surprise of discovery, and the amazing continuation of their beauty within the speaker's mind
- To identify the "inward eye" in line 21 of "I Wandered Lonely as a Cloud"
- To identify similes, personification, and particularly melodious lines
- To demonstrate an understanding of inverted word order and its relation to the poem's rhyme scheme
- To write a comparison of a prose description and a poetry description of the same scene
- To demonstrate a knowledge of specific details in "Loveliest of Trees"
- To analyze the speaker's motives for going to see the trees
- To interpret the sentence "Fifty springs are little room" in order to discern its relation to the poem's theme
- To differentiate between the implied attitudes toward nature expressed in "Loveliest of Trees" and "I Wandered Lonely as a Cloud"

READING/CRITICAL THINKING STRATEGIES

Finding Sequence

Before students begin reading "I Wandered Lonely as a Cloud," you might ask them to picture a peaceful or beautiful scene in their minds and to describe the scene, either moving from right to left, or top to bottom. Tell students that as they read this poem they should determine the spatial order they would use if painting or drawing it. What hints does Wordsworth provide to help them decide? What does he leave totally to their imaginations? As students read, ask them to map or draw the scene that Wordsworth depicts. After students have completed their reading, ask them to share their findings. Is it always true that a picture is worth more than a thousand words? When is it true that a map is worth more than a picture? When is a picture worth more than a map or a thousand words?

VOCABULARY

I Wandered Lonely as a Cloud
Pensive (line 20) and *solitude* (line 22) are defined in the glossary.

VOCABULARY ACTIVITY

Loveliest of Trees
Direct students' attention to the different ways that time is measured in the second stanza of A. E. Housman's "Loveliest of Trees." Ask the class, "Where else have you seen or heard the word *score* used to mean twenty years?" Some students should answer, "The Gettysburg Address." (To refresh students' memories, you may wish to recite the opening of the Gettysburg Address.) In line 6, Housman uses the word *twenty* rather than *a score*, and in the next line he measures his life by the seasons— "seventy springs." Engage the class in brainstorming additional ways that time is measured—for example, by hours, minutes, decades, ticks of the clock, stages of development (such as youth, adolescence, and middle age), phases of the moon, and light years. To impress upon students the great variety of time measurements, you may

continued ☞

wish to write on the chalkboard each one suggested by the class; you should be able to fill an average board in little time.

Finally, lead the class in analyzing why, of all the measurements available, Housman chose the ones that he did. What effect do Housman's choices have on the meaning, tone, rhythm, and other facets of the poem? Student answers will vary widely; be prepared to affirm any response that the student can support with a logical argument based on specific examples and cogent views.

ANSWER KEYS

STUDY GUIDE

I Wandered Lonely as a Cloud   Text Page 377
Loveliest of Trees   Text Page 379

1. The speaker is the poet. He uses the first person, *I,* and identifies himself as a poet (line 15).
2. The unexpected sight of all those beautiful daffodils changes the speaker's mood.
3. The memory of the daffodils has the power to uplift the speaker's spirits even now.
4. It is spring (Eastertide), and the speaker is overlooking a forest path with blooming cherry trees.
5. The speaker is twenty and expects to live until he is seventy.
6. The speaker concludes that he must take advantage of the spring beauty while he can.
7. The cherry blossoms are compared to snow.
8. **a.** The speaker's mood may be lonely (vacant) or serious and sad (pensive).
   b. The "inward eye," or one's memory, appears when one is alone (in solitude).
9. The poet compares the bank of daffodils to the stars of the Milky Way.
10. He describes them as dancing people.
11. Loneliness or sadness and joy
12. In each stanza, the first and third, the second and fourth, and the fifth and sixth lines rhyme.
13. Only twelve lines long, "Loveliest of Trees" is a short poem and is rich with musical devices. The poet uses rhyming couplets, alliteration, and assonance (for example, in lines 3 and 4). In just twelve lines, the poet expresses intense feelings of his own fleeting mortality as well as his joy in nature.

BUILDING VOCABULARY

O Mistress Mine   Text Page 376
I Wandered Lonely as a Cloud   Text Page 377

A. Answers may vary. Ask students to justify different answers.
1. b
2. a
3. c
4. c
5. c
6. b
7. c
8. a *or* c

B. 9.–11. Sentences will vary.

I WANDERED LONELY AS A CLOUD
and LOVELIEST OF TREES *(Pages 377–379)*

William Wordsworth (1770–1850) *and* A. E. Housman (1859–1936)

Understanding the Poems

"I Wandered Lonely as a Cloud" (Pages 377–378)

1. Identify the poem's speaker.

_____

_____

_____

2. What causes the speaker's change of mood?

_____

_____

3. What lasting benefit has the speaker received from his encounter with the daffodils?

_____

_____

"Loveliest of Trees" (Page 379)

4. Identify the poem's setting.

_____

_____

_____

5. How old is the speaker, and how long does he expect to live?

_____

_____

continued ☞

6. What conclusion does the speaker draw in the third stanza?

_____

_____

_____

7. Explain the metaphor in the last line.

_____

_____

Understanding Vocabulary

8. Find *pensive* (line 20) and *solitude* (line 22) in "I Wandered Lonely as a Cloud" and check their meanings in the glossary or in a dictionary. Then answer the following items:

a. In your own words, describe the speaker's mood as he lies on the couch (line 20).

_____

_____

b. According to the speaker, under what conditions does the "inward eye" appear (line 22)? _____

_____

Understanding Literary Elements

9. What two things does the poet compare in lines 7–8 of "I Wandered Lonely as a Cloud"?

_____

_____

10. How does the speaker personify the daffodils?

_____

_____

11. What two intense, opposite feelings are expressed in "I Wandered Lonely as a Cloud"?

_____

_____

continued ☞

12. Explain the rhyme scheme of "I Wandered Lonely as a Cloud."

_____

_____

_____

Writing and Responding to Literature

13. Explain how "Loveliest of Trees" reflects the characteristics of a lyric poem. (Refer to page 374 for these characteristics.) Use specific examples from the poem to illustrate your points.

_____

_____

_____

_____

_____

_____

_____

_____

_____

_____

_____

O Mistress Mine
I Wandered Lonely as a Cloud

William Shakespeare (Page 376)
William Wordsworth (Page 377)

———————————— ANALYZING SYNONYMS ————————————

ACTIVITY A

Synonyms are words that have the same, or almost the same, meaning, such as *tranquil* and *calm*. The dictionary entry for a word often includes a **synonymy,** a list of synonyms for the word with accompanying discussions of the various shades of meaning among the synonyms. Using a dictionary that includes synonymies in its entries, select the letter of the word that best completes each sentence below.

1. _____ The shrill noise of the car alarm _____ for more than an hour.
   a. endured   **b.** persisted   **c.** lasted

2. _____ Despite her many hardships, Sojourner Truth not only _____, but she triumphed.
   a. endured   **b.** continued   **c.** lasted

3. _____ The "troubles" in Northern Ireland have _____ for many generations.
   a. endured   **b.** abode   **c.** lasted

4. _____ Howie has been staring out the window with a _____ look on his face.
   a. reflective   **b.** contemplative   **c.** pensive

5. _____ I spent a quiet, _____ half hour in the chapel before making my final decision.
   a. pensive   **b.** meditative   **c.** reflective

6. _____ In some hospitals, patients with very contagious diseases are kept in _____ from other patients.
   a. solitude   **b.** isolation   **c.** seclusion

7. _____ Laurie says that she enjoys the _____ of a rainy day alone with a good book and good music.
   a. solitude   **b.** isolation   **c.** seclusion

8. _____ During her period of complete _____, Jane Goodall wrote a book about her observations of gorillas.
   a. solitude   **b.** isolation   **c.** seclusion

continued ☞

ACTIVITY B

Use each of the following words in an original sentence.

9. *endured* _____

_____

10. *pensive* _____

_____

11. *solitude* _____

_____

TEACHER'S NOTES

DESERT PLACES   *Robert Frost*   Text Page 380
RECESSIONAL   *Rudyard Kipling*   Text Page 381

OBJECTIVES   The aims of this lesson are for the student:
- To identify specific details that contribute to poetic mood in "Desert Places"
- To express and interpret the mood evoked in the first two stanzas of Frost's poem
- To demonstrate an understanding of the meaning of lines 7 and 8 of "Desert Places"
- To identify the future changes foreseen by the speaker of "Desert Places"
- To analyze the phrase "own desert places" in order to express its relation to the poem's theme
- To identify the sources of power presented in "Recessional" and explain Kipling's view of each
- To indicate passages in "Recessional" that stress the insufficiency of warfare in maintaining national greatness
- To analyze the connections between the expansion of empire, national pride, and the decay of national power in Kipling's poem
- To demonstrate recognition of instances of a refrain in Kipling's poem
- To demonstrate a knowledge of how Kipling alters the standard form of the "refrain"

VOCABULARY   ***Desert Places***
Lair(s) (line 6) is defined in the glossary.
The following words are defined in the glossary:

Recessional		reek (ing)	(26)
tumult	**(7)**	**valiant**	**(27)**
contrite	**(10)**	**frantic**	**(29)**

ANSWER KEYS

STUDY GUIDE

1. The poem takes place in the evening as the speaker passes a field that is filling up with snow.
2. The speaker seems lonely, desolate, depressed, preoccupied, almost alienated from his surroundings.
3. *It* refers to the field. The sentence means that the field belongs to the surrounding woods.
4. As desolate as the field is, it will become more desolate as the snow fills it completely and covers the remaining stubble. When it becomes white, it will have no expression, and there will be nothing for it to express because all of it will be covered.

5. According to the speaker, desert places exist (1) in the snow-covered field, (2) between and on stars, and (3) within himself.
6. Line 4
7. The speaker asks God to remain with, to spare, and to be merciful to the British Empire.
8. The speaker is bothered and concerned.
9. Since it is winter, all the wild animals are hibernating in their dens.
10. a. They might refer to the actual celebrations of the Jubilee or to the boasts that accompany Britain's celebration of power.
    b. The speaker indicates that a heart that is modest and knows its own weaknesses and shortcomings will last.

continued ☞

c. The gun is long and thin and hollow like a tube. It smokes or reeks after it is fired.

d. All three words have negative connotations.

e. Although *valiant* means brave, *dust* gives an overriding feeling of impermanence.

11. Students' opinions will vary. It seems that Kipling wanted to offer some counterbalance to the celebration. In the midst of celebrating its power, he did not want Britain to become too confident or careless. He wanted to lend some perspective to the celebration, to remind his countrymen of what is truly important and lasting.

BUILDING VOCABULARY

A. Answers will vary. Sample answers are provided.
  1. SYNONYM: commotion ANTONYM: peace
  2. SYNONYM: repentant ANTONYM: unrepentant
  3. SYNONYM: brave ANTONYM: cowardly
  4. SYNONYM: frenzied ANTONYM: calm
  5. SYNONYM: splendor ANTONYM: simplicity

B. Answers will vary. Sample answers are provided.
  6. a. Answers will vary. Students may suggest presidential inaugurations, royal weddings, dedications of national monuments, and other lavish or official occasions.
    b. Most students will probably answer that they would not be pleased because *pompous* carries the meaning of "arrogant; excessively or overly self-important."
  7. Answers will vary.
  8. a. Most students will answer that they would not accept an invitation into a lion's den.
    b. In forests, mountains, and other wild natural environments, and in zoos and wildlife parks
  9. Answers will vary, but all should be trying, hectic, troubling, anxious situations.
  10. a. The people who are governed.
    b. An absolute sovereign who has a hereditary claim to rule
    c. A single person or a small ruling clique
  11. Answers will vary.

Study Guide

DESERT PLACES *and* RECESSIONAL (*Pages 380–382*)

Robert Frost (1874–1963) *and* Rudyard Kipling (1865–1936)

Understanding the Poems

"Desert Places" (Page 380)

1. When and where does this poem take place?

   _____

   _____

   _____

2. Describe the poem's speaker.

   _____

   _____

   _____

3. To what does the word *it* in line 5 refer?

   _____

   _____

4. Restate the ideas of the third stanza in your own words.

   _____

   _____

   _____

   _____

5. In what three places does the speaker say "desert places" exist?

   _____

   _____

   _____

continued ☞

"Recessional" (Pages 381–382)

6. What line in the first stanza suggests the vastness of the British empire?

_____

_____

7. At the end of each stanza, the speaker makes a request of God. For what does the speaker ask?

_____

_____

8. Describe the speaker's tone in the last stanza.

_____

_____

Understanding Vocabulary

9. Find *lair(s)* (line 6) in "Desert Places" and check its meaning in the glossary or in a dictionary. In your own words, explain the image created in line 6.

_____

_____

10. Find *tumult* (line 7), *contrite* (line 10), *reek(ing)* (line 26), *valiant* (line 27), and *frantic* (line 29) in "Recessional" and check their meanings in the glossary or in a dictionary. Then respond to the following items:

a. To what might the tumult and shouting of line 7 refer? _____

_____

_____

b. In your own words, describe what the speaker says will last in line 10. _____

_____

_____

_____

continued ☞

c. Explain the speaker's image of "reeking tube" to describe a gun. _____

_____

_____

d. Do *frantic, boast,* and *foolish* in line 29 have negative, positive, or mixed connotations?

_____

_____

e. Does the phrase "valiant dust" (line 27) suggest a permanent or impermanent image?

_____

_____

Writing and Responding to Literature

11. In your opinion, why did Kipling write such a somber poem for a time of rejoicing?

_____

_____

_____

_____

_____

_____

_____

_____

_____

NAME _____

CLASS _____ DATE _____ SCORE _____

Desert Places · *Robert Frost* · (Page 380)
Recessional · *Rudyard Kipling* · (Page 381)

———————— **WRITING SYNONYMS AND ANTONYMS / APPLYING DEFINITIONS** ————————

Synonyms are words that have the same, or almost the same, meaning, such as *tranquil* and *calm, nourish* and *feed, frying pan* and *skillet.* **Antonyms** are words that have opposite meanings, such as *twilight* and *dawn, clumsy* and *graceful, arrive* and *depart.*

ACTIVITY A

Using a thesaurus, supply a synonym and an antonym for each of the words listed below.

SYNONYM · ANTONYM

1. *tumult* _____ _____

2. *contrite* _____ _____

3. *valiant* _____ _____

4. *frantic* _____ _____

5. *pomp* _____ _____

ACTIVITY B

Using a dictionary, complete the following items.

6. a. List some occasions that you associate with *pomp.*

_____

b. How would you feel if someone called you *pompous*? Explain. _____

_____

_____

7. Describe a *valiant* act that you have witnessed or read about. _____

_____

_____

continued ☞

8. a. If a lion invited you into his *lair,* would you go? Explain. _____

_____

   b. Where would you most likely find a bear's *lair?* _____

_____

9. Describe a situation in which you would feel *frantic.* _____

_____

_____

10. Who has *dominion* in each of the following forms of government?

   a. a democracy _____

   b. a monarchy _____

   c. a dictatorship _____

11. Describe a situation in which you felt *contrite.* _____

_____

_____

TEACHER'S NOTES

LORD RANDAL   *Anonymous*

Text Page 384

ALL IN GREEN WENT MY LOVE RIDING

E. E. Cummings

Text Page 386

OBJECTIVES

The aims of this lesson are for the student:

- To draw inferences from textual clues in order to speculate about what has happened to Lord Randal
- To analyze Lord Randal's motivations for not immediately telling his mother that he is sick
- To interpret the symbolic meaning of Lord Randal's sickness "at the heart"
- To identify instances of repetition and alliteration in "Lord Randal"
- To identify the refrain of "Lord Randal"
- To analyze the relationship between the changing refrain and the escalating tension of "Lord Randal"
- To identify specific details of Cummings' poem that establish the narrative's time setting
- To analyze the similarities and dissimilarities between Cummings' poem and traditional ballads
- To analyze the creation of a tone of mystery by the visual imagery of this poem
- To identify abrupt shifts of scene in "All in green went my love riding"
- To interpret the hunter/hunted relation of this poem in order to demonstrate an understanding of the poem's theme
- To draw inferences from this poem's use of a refrain as to the poem's theme
- To freewrite notes on the connotations of phrases in Cummings' poem

SUMMARY

Lord Randal

"Lord Randal" tells the story of a young man who has been poisoned by his sweetheart. When he comes home one evening, his mother asks him where he has been. He tells her he has been hunting in the wood and wants to lie down. His mother continues to question him, and he reveals that he had a dinner of boiled eels with his sweetheart. He says that his bloodhounds, who probably ate the scraps, swelled and died, prompting his mother to guess that he has been poisoned. The poem ends with Lord Randal sick at heart and in body.

All in green went my love riding

The speaker in the poem, a woman, describes her lover's morning hunt. Using his sinister hounds, he flushes and kills several deer, doe and buck alike. The last two lines indicate, depending on the reader's interpretation, that the speaker is hunted and killed by her love, or that she has been pursued and won by a man whose cruel nature she had not seen before.

READING/CRITICAL THINKING STRATEGIES

Interpreting

Before students begin reading "All in green went my love riding," you might tell them that in medieval ballads, the words *hunting, chasing,* and *capturing* are all associated with love. You might ask if any similar language is employed today when discussing romance—do people still capture each other's hearts, for instance? Tell students that as they read this poem they should consider it first at a literal level. You may want to have students paraphrase each stanza. After students have completed their reading, ask them to compare their paraphrases and to discuss how the poem might be interpreted, particularly the last line.

continued ☞

Song	Paraphrase
Stanza 1	At dawn my love, dressed in green, went riding on a large gold horse.
Stanza 2	

VOCABULARY *All in green went my love riding*
Lithe (line 17), *famished* (line 20), and *sheer* (line 25) are defined in the glossary.

VOCABULARY ACTIVITY

In stanzas 3, 7, and 11 in "All in green went my love riding," E. E. Cummings uses pairs of adjectives to describe deer. Lead the class in analyzing each pair to discover how the adjectives reinforce and complement one another. For example, "swift sweet deer" (line 7) refers to the speed and beauty or disposition of the deer, while "red rare" (line 8) refers to the deer's color and exquisite appearance. As the class suggests synonymous words and phrases for each adjective, write them on the chalkboard. Then select closely related synonyms and ask for volunteers to identify in what ways they are similar and dissimilar.

Continue this analysis by extending the discussion to single words and phrases in the poem, such as "crouched," "dappled," "slippered sleep," "famished arrow," and "daunting death." Again, have students give synonymous words and phrases and then analyze similarities and differences between selected pairs.

Conclude the discussion by having each student choose an image in the poem— such as the phrase in the title, "four lean hounds crouched low and smiling," "the level meadows ran before," or "riding the mountain down"—and write a short report analyzing the separate words in the phrase and their relationships with each other. Suggest to students that before they begin writing, they follow the procedure used in the class discussion and closely examine synonyms of the words in the phrase. Request that the reports end with a short discussion of why Cummings chose the words that he did rather than any of the synonymous words or phrases that students identify.

You can collect these reports as either graded or ungraded homework assignments, and you may wish to have students who have written particularly clever or insightful reports present them to the class.

ANSWER KEYS

STUDY GUIDE

Lord Randal   Text Page 384
All in green went my love riding   Text Page 386

1. The bloodhounds swelled and died. The implication is that the dogs, as well as their master, ate some of the poison. Their deaths foreshadow Lord Randal's.

2. The last line suggests that Lord Randal realizes that he was poisoned by his sweetheart, possibly as the result of a lover's quarrel.

3. The speaker is a woman who watches her love go hunting for deer.

4. Twelve

5. The speaker's love hunts with a golden horse, four hounds, a horn, and a bow and arrow.

6. The deer's description is sympathetic. The speaker calls them *sweet, rare,* and *tense.*

7. The hounds' description is sinister. They seem to enjoy the prospect of hunting and killing. "Crouched low and smiling" suggests they are eager to hunt.

8. The speaker

9. The hunter may have killed the speaker.

10. The speaker's love or feelings for the hunter might be dead.

11.   **a.** He personifies the arrow when he calls it *famished.*

     b. Sheer peaks would be very steep mountains that would be difficult to climb.

     c. Deer run and jump easily and swiftly.

continued ☞

12. "Lord Randal my son," lines 1, 5, 9, 13, 17; "my handsome young man," lines 2, 6, 10, 14, 18; "mother, make my bed soon," lines 3, 7, 11, 15, 19; and "For I'm weary wi' hunting, and fain wald lie down," lines 4, 8, 12, 16, modified in 20.

13. Folk ballads have been passed orally from generation to generation.

14. A ballad (1) is composed of four-lined rhymed stanzas, (2) employs strong and simple rhythm, (3) frequently employs dialogues, (4) focuses upon one dramatic or tragic incident, and (5) may shift scenes rapidly.

15. "Lord Randal" is an anonymous ballad of folk origin. Its repetitions and refrain make it particularly suitable for singing. It is written in four-lined rhymed stanzas and maintains a simple, strong rhythm. The story involves the tragic murder of Lord Randal by his lover. It is told entirely through dialogue and leaves gaps in the story, such as the explicit motive for murder.

BUILDING VOCABULARY

All in green went my love riding   Text Page 386

1. hunger
2. to starve to death
3. famishment
4. Sentences will vary.
5. adjective, adverb, and noun
6. definition number 4
7. steep
8. Sentences will vary.
9. sheerly
10. flexible, supple, limber, lissome
11. soft, mild
12. Sentences will vary.

Study Guide

LORD RANDAL *and* **All in green went my love riding** *(Pages 384–387)*

Anonymous *and* **e. e. cummings** (1894–1962)

Understanding the Poems

"Lord Randal" (Page 384)

1. Explain what happened to Lord Randal's bloodhounds and the significance of this event.

_____

_____

_____

2. What does the last line suggest about Lord Randal's murderer?

_____

_____

_____

"All in green went my love riding" (Pages 386–387)

3. Identify the poem's speaker.

_____

_____

4. By the end of the poem, how many deer has the hunter killed? _____

5. With what does the speaker's love go hunting?

_____

_____

6. How are the deer described?

_____

_____

continued ☞

7. How are the hounds described?

_____

_____

_____

8. Who seems to be the hunter's final victim? _____

_____

9. Explain how the final line might be literally true.

_____

_____

10. Explain how the final line might be figuratively true.

_____

_____

Understanding Vocabulary

11. Find *lithe* (line 17), *famish(ed)* (line 20), and *sheer* (line 25) in "All in green went my love riding" and check their meanings in the glossary or in a dictionary. Then respond to the following items:

a. When he calls the arrow famished, what figure of speech does the poet create? _____

_____

_____

b. Describe *sheer* peaks. _____

_____

_____

c. Why would the poet describe the deer as lithe? _____

_____

_____

Understanding Literary Elements

12. Identify the phrases that are repeated in "Lord Randal."

_____

_____

_____

_____

13. What accounts for the different versions of a folk ballad?

_____

_____

14. List the characteristics of a ballad.

_____

_____

_____

_____

Writing and Responding to Literature

15. Explain how "Lord Randal" displays the characteristics of a folk ballad. Use examples from the poem to illustrate your points.

_____

_____

_____

_____

_____

_____

_____

Building Vocabulary

All in green went my love riding   *E. E. Cummings*   *(Page 386)*

―――――――――――――――― UNDERSTANDING DICTIONARY ENTRIES ――――――――――――――――

ACTIVITY

A **dictionary entry** gives a great deal of information about a word. You may look up a word to find its pronunciation, meaning, origin, part of speech, and its plural and related forms. Use the following entries from *Webster's New World Dictionary* to complete the items below.

> **fam·ish** (-ish) *vt., vi.* [ME. *famishen*, altered (after verbs ending in *-ish-*: cf. CHERISH) < *famen*, aphetic < OFr. *afamer* < VL. **affamare* < L. *ad*, to + *fames*, hunger: see prec.] **1.** to make or be very hungry; make or become weak from hunger **2.** [Obs.] to starve to death—**fam′ish·ment** *n.*

> **lithe** (līth) *adj.* [ME. < OE. *lithe*, soft, mild, akin to OHG. *lindi* < IE. base **lento-*, flexible, bendable, whence L. *lentus*, pliant, flexible & LINDEN] bending easily; flexible; supple; limber; lissome: also **lithe′some** (-səm)—**lithe′ly** *adv.*—**lithe′ness** *n.*

> **sheer²** (shir) *adj.* [ME. *schere*, prob. var. of *scere*, free, exempt < ON. *skærr*, bright, clear, akin to G. *schier:* for IE. base see SHINE] **1.** very thin; transparent; diaphanous: said of textiles **2.** not mixed or mingled with anything else; pure [*sheer* ice] **3.** absolute; downright; unqualified; utter [*sheer* persistence] **4.** perpendicular or extremely steep, as the face of a cliff—*adv.* **1.** completely; utterly; outright **2.** perpendicularly or very steeply—*n.* thin, fine material, or a garment made of it—*SYN.* see STEEP¹—**sheer′ly** *adv.*—**sheer′ness** *n.*

1. What does the Latin word *fames* mean? _____

2. What is an obsolete meaning of *famish*? _____

3. What is the noun form of *famish*? _____

4. Write an original sentence using *famished*. _____

_____

5. The entry gives meanings for *sheer* when used as three different parts of speech. What

are these parts of speech? _____

6. Write the number of the definition of *sheer* as it is used in the following sentence: The

waterfall was a *sheer* drop of two hundred yards. _____

7. Write a synonym for *sheer*. _____

continued ☞

8. Write a sentence using *sheer* as an adjective in the sense of definition number 2.

_____

_____

9. Write the adverbial form of *sheer*. _____

10. Write four synonyms for *lithe*. _____

_____

11. What does the Old English word *lithe* mean? _____

12. Write an original sentence using *lithe*. _____

_____

TEACHER'S NOTES

THE CASTLE   *Edwin Muir*   Text Page 389
THE SEVEN AGES OF MAN   *William Shakespeare*   Text Page 391

OBJECTIVES   The aims of this lesson are for the student:
- To identify the reasons for the castle's inhabitants' confidence, and the events leading to their downfall
- To demonstrate an understanding of the fifth stanza of "The Castle," particularly the word "cause" and the phrase "without a groan"
- To infer why the poet does not give the narrative a specific locale
- To draw inferences from specific lines as to the poem's moral
- To restate the moral of "The Castle" in the student's own words
- To draw inferences from Jaques' description as to the unpleasant futility of life
- To identify instances of comedy in Shakespeare's monologue
- To interpret the tone of Jaques' description of the seventh and last age of man
- To analyze metaphor, simile, and other figurative language in order to demonstrate an understanding of how it helps to reveal Jaques' attitudes
- To analyze and evaluate an artist's interpretation of a poem

SUMMARY   "The Castle" tells the story of an unspecified battle. The speaker is one of several men lodged in a seemingly impenetrable castle. They have plenty of arms and food; their allies are nearby; the castle gates are strong; and the walls are high, thick, and smooth. Yet these men are defeated when the enemy bribes one of their own, the warder, who lets the enemy soldiers through a little gate.

READING/CRITICAL THINKING STRATEGIES

Finding Significant Details
Before students begin reading "The Castle," ask if they know of any stories in which someone betrays a friend or family or country for money. Encourage students to share some of the stories. Tell students that the poem they are about to read is similar to those stories. Suggest that as students read they take note of the reasons the people in the castle feel secure. After students have finished their reading, ask them to compare their findings and to discuss their reactions to the last two lines. Is the only enemy gold? Are these lines to be taken literally?

VOCABULARY   The following words are defined in the glossary:

The Castle		tier	(8)
provender	(7)	treacherous	(22)
battlement (s)	(8)		

The Seven Ages of Man
Puke (–ing) (line 6), *satchel* (line 7), and *treble* (line 24) are defined in the glossary.

continued 👉

The Seven Ages of Man

Solving analogies helps students build vocabulary skills by providing practice with categorizing, interpreting context clues, differentiating between shades of meaning, examining relationships between words and concepts, and applying a number of other basic techniques for determining the meanings of unfamiliar words. To help students master unfamiliar words in "The Seven Ages of Man," present the following incomplete analogies to the class and have students fill in each blank with an appropriate word. If you have identified other words that have given students difficulty, you may wish to create analogies for those words and add them to this list.

1. tunes : songs :: saws : _____

2. gathering : dispersing :: mewling : _____

3. up : rise :: sans : _____

4. agility : gracefulness :: oblivion : _____

5. arm : hand :: shank : _____

Answers [These are possible answers; student answers will likely vary.]

1. sayings. Tunes are songs; saws are sayings.
2. laughing. *Gathering* and *dispersing* are antonyms, as are *mewling* and *laughing*.
3. lack. *Up* refers to the rise of something; *sans* refers to the lack of something.
4. forgetfulness. *Agility* and *gracefulness* are synonyms, as are *oblivion* and *forgetfulness*.
5. foot. An arm has a hand at the end of it; a shank (leg) has a foot at the end of it.

If you have not presented analogies to your class before, look at the tips for doing so given under the **Vocabulary Activity** heading for Claude McKay's "A Song of the Moon" in this booklet.

ANSWER KEYS

STUDY GUIDE A

The Castle   Text Page 389

1. The speaker is one of the betrayed soldiers of the castle.
2. Even though the setting suggests conflict, the speaker describes his fellow soldiers as at ease. The inhabitants of the surrounding countryside go about their own (peaceful) business (mowing hay). The soldiers can see their enemy from the tower and keep track of any movement they make.
3. This line suggests that the speaker was very confident.
4. Gold
5. The speaker calls the gate *little, private,* and *wicked.* He describes the warder as *wizened,* suggesting he was old and small.
6. a. The castle was well stocked with weapons and provisions in case there was a siege or long attack. The castle walls were strong and built for defense.
   b. After the betrayal and enemy invasion, the stone walls were no longer a reliable source of protection.
7. The speaker tells his story for two reasons. First, he feels that he has nothing about which to be ashamed concerning the defeat. Second, he tells the story as a warning to others to beware of possible betrayal from every source.

STUDY GUIDE B

The Seven Ages of Man   Text Page 391

1. The speaker compares life to a play.
2. The stages of life are compared to the acts of a play.
3. a. crying and throwing up
   b. whining and unwilling to go to school
   c. sighing and making ballads
   d. quarrelsome and jealous
   e. heavy-set, full of obvious wisdom and sayings
   f. shrunken in form, foolish, wearing spectacles
   g. oblivious; without teeth, eyesight, a sense of taste, or anything else

continued ☞

4. The lover is described as "sighing like a furnace," which suggests that he is overexcited and that his feelings are excessive. The sorrowful ballad that the lover writes is in praise of his lover's eyebrow, not a common subject for a ballad of love.

5. The speaker seems to think that reputation is easily lost and is not very important. He says it is a bubble, which will burst easily.

6. In both stages, the person is helpless; and in both, the person has no teeth and either inadequate or undeveloped sensory perceptions.

7. Jaques' outlook on life is basically gloomy and pessimistic.

8. **a.** It carries negative connotations.
   b. The schoolboy with his bookbag and fresh, bright face moves slowly and reluctantly to school.
   c. The man's voice becomes high-pitched again like a child's and is accompanied by wheezes and sighs.

9. Students' answers will vary.

BUILDING VOCABULARY

The Castle	Text Page 389
The Seven Ages of Man	Text Page 391

The words that students underline and the wording of definitions will vary. Suggested definitions are provided. Sentences will also vary.

1. *provender:* food for livestock; food
2. *battlements:* walls with open spaces to shoot through

3. *tier:* a layer
4. *treacherous:* disloyal
5. *satchel:* small suitcase
6. *treble:* high-pitched voice
7. *allies:* countries, groups, or people joined together for a common purpose

SELECTION VOCABULARY TEST

Psalm 96	Text Page 345
Art Review	Text Page 364
O Mistress Mine	Text Page 376
I Wandered Lonely as a Cloud	Text Page 377
Desert Places	Text Page 380
Recessional	Text Page 381
All in green went my love riding	Text Page 386
The Castle	Text Page 389
The Seven Ages of Man	Text Page 391

A.

1.	k	9.	b
2.	d	10.	p
3.	h	11.	f
4.	o	12.	n
5.	a	13.	j
6.	l	14.	g
7.	i	15.	m
8.	e		

B.

1.	b	4.	f
2.	d	5.	e
3.	a		

NAME _____

CLASS _____ DATE _____ SCORE _____

THE CASTLE   *(Page 389)*

Edwin Muir *(1887–1959)*

Understanding the Poem

1. Identify the poem's speaker.

_____

_____

2. What images in the first stanza suggest a feeling of security?

_____

_____

_____

_____

_____

3. What does line 15 suggest about the speaker's attitude?

_____

_____

_____

4. What was the warder's motive for betrayal? _____

_____

5. With what words does the speaker describe the wicket gate and the warder?

_____

_____

_____

_____

continued ☞

Understanding Vocabulary

6. Find *provender* (line 7), *battlement(s)* (line 8), *tier* (line 8), and *treacherous* (line 22) in the poem and check their meanings in the glossary or in a dictionary. Then respond to the following items:

   a. Explain in your own words the speaker's reasons (lines 7–8) for feeling secure. _____

   _____

   _____

   _____

   b. Why does the speaker call the stone walls treacherous? _____

   _____

   _____

Writing and Responding to Literature

7. The speaker of "The Castle" calls his story shameful. According to the last stanza, what is his motivation for telling it?

   _____

   _____

   _____

   _____

   _____

   _____

   _____

NAME _____

CLASS _____ DATE _____ SCORE _____

THE SEVEN AGES OF MAN   *(Pages 391–392)*

William Shakespeare (1564–1616)

Understanding the Poem

1. To what does the speaker compare life?

_____

_____

2. To what are the stages of life compared?

_____

_____

3. Briefly describe each stage of life as outlined by the poem's speaker.

   a. _____

   _____

   b. _____

   _____

   c. _____

   _____

   d. _____

   _____

   e. _____

   _____

   f. _____

   _____

   g. _____

   _____

continued ☞

4. What is amusing about the speaker's description of the "lover stage" (lines 9–11)?

_____

_____

_____

_____

5. In line 14, what is the speaker's opinion about gaining a reputation?

_____

_____

_____

6. How is the last stage of life like the first?

_____

_____

_____

7. Describe the speaker's basic outlook on life.

_____

_____

Understanding Vocabulary

8. Find *puke(-ing)* (line 6), *satchel* (line 7), and *treble* (line 24) in the poem and check their meanings in the glossary or in a dictionary. Then respond to the following items:

a. Does the description of the infant in line 6 carry negative, positive, or mixed

connotations? _____

_____

b. In your own words, describe the schoolboy's image, lines 7–8. _____

_____

_____

c. Describe the man's voice in his sixth age when it turns "again toward childish treble"

(line 24). _____

_____

_____

Writing and Responding to Literature

9. Do you agree with Jaques that life occurs in the seven stages he identifies? Explain why you agree or disagree.

_____

_____

_____

_____

_____

_____

_____

_____

_____

Building Vocabulary

NAME _____

CLASS _____ DATE _____ SCORE _____

The Castle
The Seven Ages of Man

Edwin Muir   (Page 389)

William Shakespeare   (Page 391)

—————— **USING CONTEXT CLUES / USING WORDS IN CONTEXT** ——————

ACTIVITY

Sometimes you can guess the meaning of an unfamiliar word from its **context**—the words, phrases, and sentences that surround it. The context may provide an example, a definition, or some other clue to the word's meaning. In each of the numbered items, underline the context clue for the italicized word. Then make a guess at the word's meaning. Check your guess in a dictionary, and write a definition for the italicized word. Finally, use the italicized word in a sentence.

1. He purchased a large bag of oats as *provender* for his horse.

    MEANING _____

    SENTENCE _____

    _____

2. Armed soldiers stood watch on the *battlements* atop each of the castle's six towers.

    MEANING _____

    SENTENCE _____

    _____

3. The top *tier* of the wedding cake featured a miniature bride and groom. The other layers were decorated with fresh flowers.

    MEANING _____

    SENTENCE _____

    _____

4. Everyone condemned the spy's *treacherous* act: he had sold his nation's most precious secrets to an enemy.

    MEANING _____

    SENTENCE _____

    _____

continued ☞

5. A briefcase is a small *satchel* for carrying books and papers.

MEANING _____

SENTENCE _____

_____

6. The soprano's wavering *treble* ruined the aria; she was not able to hit the high notes demanded by the composer.

MEANING _____

SENTENCE _____

_____

7. During World War II, the *allies* who joined together to fight Germany were Great Britain, the United States, and the Soviet Union.

MEANING _____

SENTENCE _____

_____

Psalm 96	from *The King James Bible*	*(Page 345)*
Art Review	*Kenneth Fearing*	*(Page 364)*
O Mistress Mine	*William Shakespeare*	*(Page 376)*
I Wandered Lonely as a Cloud	*William Wordsworth*	*(Page 377)*
Desert Places	*Robert Frost*	*(Page 380)*
Recessional	*Rudyard Kipling*	*(Page 381)*
All in green went my love riding	*E. E. Cummings*	*(Page 386)*
The Castle	*Edwin Muir*	*(Page 389)*
The Seven Ages of Man	*William Shakespeare*	*(Page 391)*

───── VOCABULARY TEST ─────

A. Match each word in column I with the correct definition in column II. Place the letter of each definition you choose in the space provided. (5 points each)

I	II
_____ 1. tumult	**a.** excessively emotional
_____ 2. contrite	**b.** food
_____ 3. reek	**c.** coming from the sun
_____ 4. valiant	**d.** feeling guilty for wrongdoing
_____ 5. frantic	**e.** very steep
_____ 6. lithe	**f.** one of a series or layers
_____ 7. famished	**g.** a small suitcase or bag
_____ 8. sheer	**h.** to give off smoke or odors
_____ 9. provender	**i.** starving
_____ 10. battlement	**j.** to vomit
_____ 11. tier	**k.** great noise; emotional disturbance
_____ 12. treacherous	**l.** limber
_____ 13. puke	**m.** a high-pitched voice
_____ 14. satchel	**n.** unreliable; dangerous; disloyal
_____ 15. treble	**o.** brave
	p. a wall with open spaces to shoot through

continued ☞

B. In the space provided, write the letter of the word taken from the list below which is closest in meaning to the italicized synonym or definition in each of the following sentences. (10 points each)

a. pensive	**c.** idol	**e.** lairs
b. morbid	**d.** endure	**f.** solitude

_____ **1.** Some writing on walls is (*gruesome*).

_____ **2.** Shakespeare tells us that youth does not (*last*).

_____ **3.** Wordsworth says that he is often (*thoughtful*).

_____ **4.** Wordsworth says that he remembers the daffodils in his (*aloneness*).

_____ **5.** Frost says that all the animals are in their (*homes of wild animals*).

TEACHER'S NOTES

UPHILL	*Christina Rossetti*	Text Page 394
THE ERL-KING	*Johann Wolfgang von Goethe*	Text Page 395

OBJECTIVES The aims of this lesson are for the student:
- To interpret specific textual clues in order to demonstrate an understanding of the symbolic meaning of "Uphill"
- To describe the questioner's and the answerer's tones in "Uphill"
- To analyze the poet's manipulation of line length, indentation, and punctuation to create a sense of there being two speakers
- To identify the poem's rhyme scheme and how it identifies the poem's speakers
- To demonstrate an understanding of the poem's title
- To interpret the significance of the child's awareness of the Erl-King's presence while the father is unaware of it
- To identify the point at which the father senses danger, and his reaction to his child's fear
- To analyze the Erl-King's frightening promises to the boy
- To analyze the poem's creation of a mysteriously supernatural atmosphere
- To analyze and evaluate a composer's interpretation of Goethe's poem

ANSWER KEYS

STUDY GUIDE

Uphill	Text Page 394
The Erl-King	Text Page 395

1. The two speakers or characters are the questioner and the answerer. The questioner is someone just starting out on the road of life. The answerer may be someone older with more experience, someone who has already completed the trip, or a supernatural being.

2. In each stanza, the questioner speaks the first and third lines and the answerer speaks the second and fourth lines.

3. The first speaker is questioning and concerned about what he or she might find. The second speaker is calm, positive, and definite in the answers he or she gives.

4. The narrator, the father, the boy, and the Erl-King all speak.

5. The narrator's lines are not placed within quotation marks. The poet indicates in parentheses when the Erl-King speaks. The child and the father always address each other directly in conversation (see lines 5–6).

6. Each character's words reveal the following: the boy is frightened; the Erl-King is determined and frightening; the father is disbelieving at first and then terrified.

7. Rossetti's metaphor for life is a constant uphill journey. This view differs from Burns's view and that of many other poets who see life as a struggle to reach a peak or summit and then as a decline that is at least easier to travel. Rossetti's view suggests a life of continual struggle and toil toward a goal that is only reached at life's end. Because of the religious overtones, Rossetti's journey may also be continually uphill since it is moving upward, toward heaven.

continued ☞

SELECTION TEST

1. d
2. c
3. b
4. d
5. b
6. c
7. a
8. c
9. d
10. b

11. a
12. c
13. a
14. d
15. a
16. c
17. b
18. a
19. c
20. d

NAME _____

CLASS _____ DATE _____ SCORE _____

UPHILL and THE ERL-KING   *(Pages 394–396)*

Christina Rossetti (1830–1894) *and* Johann Wolfgang von Goethe (1749–1832)

Understanding the Poems

"Uphill" (Page 394)

1. Identify the poem's two speakers.

_____

_____

_____

_____

_____

2. In each stanza, who speaks the first and third lines? The second and fourth lines?

_____

_____

_____

3. What is the tone of each speaker in the poem?

_____

_____

_____

"The Erl-King" (Pages 395–396)

4. Name the speakers in this poem.

_____

_____

continued ☞

5. How does the poet help his readers to distinguish the words of the poem's four speakers?

_____

_____

_____

_____

6. What does the language of each character reveal about his feelings?

_____

_____

_____

Writing and Responding to Literature

7. In "John Anderson My Jo," Robert Burns's metaphor for life is a journey to the top of a hill and then down. How does Christina Rossetti's metaphor for life differ from Burns's? What does this difference suggest about her views of life and death?

_____

_____

_____

_____

_____

_____

_____

_____

_____

_____

For information regarding permissioned material included on this page, see pages ii–iv.

HRW material copyrighted under notice appearing earlier in this work.

Types of Poetry   (Page 374)

AN OPEN-BOOK TEST

Understanding Poetry.   Write the letter of the *best* answer to each question.
(*5 points each*)

1. "John Anderson My Jo" is all of the following *except*
   a. a poem in dialect   **c.** a tribute
   b. a love poem   **d.** an epitaph   1. _____

2. Burns's poem utilizes all of the following *except*
   a. a refrain   **c.** onomatopoeia
   b. parallelism   **d.** similes   2. _____

3. "O Mistress Mine" indicates that the speaker's mistress is all of the following
   except
   a. still young   **c.** quite attractive
   b. newly married   **d.** coy or cautious   3. _____

4. "I Wandered Lonely as a Cloud" contains several examples of contrast.
   Which of the following is *not* one of them?
   a. Lonely solitude and happy company
   b. Then and now
   c. Action and inaction
   d. Dancing and walking   4. _____

5. The phrase "inward eye" in Wordsworth's poem can *best* be identified as
   a. alert awareness   **c.** one's conscience
   b. thought or reflection   **d.** a good memory   5. _____

6. "Loveliest of Trees" is based on a specific attitude and a few facts. Which of
   the following is *not* one of the poem's basic facts?
   a. The speaker is enthralled with the blossoms of spring.
   b. The cherry trees are presently in full bloom.
   c. The speaker for fifty years has enjoyed the spring.
   d. The blossoming cherry trees look snow-covered.   6. _____

7. In "Desert Places," the prevailing mood is one of
   a. desolation   **c.** boredom
   b. confusion   **d.** annoyance   7. _____

8. According to Robert Frost, "desert places" exist in all of the following *except*
   a. spaces between stars   **c.** the snow
   b. the poet himself   **d.** the woods   8. _____

9. The first stanza of "Recessional" contains or implies all of the following
   except
   a. an approving God   **c.** a refrain
   b. an urgent plea   **d.** a proud boast   9. _____

continued ☞

10. The mood of the final stanza of "Recessional" is which of the following?
  a. Calm confidence
  b. Troubled doubt and concern
  c. Serene pride
  d. Humble apology   10. _____

11. We can conclude that the young man in "Lord Randal" is most stricken at the thought that his
  a. true-love has poisoned him
  b. true-love has been poisoned
  c. favorite hounds are dead
  d. mother is suspicious and worried   11. _____

12. The final line of "Lord Randal" suggests or implies which of the following?
  a. A lovers' quarrel
  b. A mild sickness
  c. A wish for death
  d. An exhausting day   12. _____

13. "All in green went my love riding" is a sophisticated modern ballad that resembles a folk ballad such as "Lord Randal" most obviously in its use of all of the following *except*
  a. a remote time
  b. a refrain
  c. concern with hunting
  d. death for the main character   13. _____

14. All of the following statements about Cummings' poem are true, or probably true *except* one. Which one?
  a. The speaker's love enjoys hunting.
  b. The lover goes hunting three times.
  c. The time is not the present.
  d. The speaker is accidentally killed.   14. _____

15. The lesson to be drawn from "The Castle" is that there is no known way to
  a. fight treachery
  b. win a war
  c. be wholly safe
  d. save one's own life   15. _____

16. In "The Castle" the statement "Our only enemy was gold" can *best* be paraphrased as
  a. "We had too much gold in our vaults."
  b. "Our enemies were too rich."
  c. "Money bought our destruction."
  d. "The richer contestant wins a war."   16. _____

17. "The Seven Ages of Man" says what about women?
  a. They are merely spectators.
  b. They too are "players."
  c. They never grow childish.
  d. They have only three "ages."   17. _____

18. The phrase "bubble reputation" (line 14) suggests that a reputation is
  a. short-lived
  b. fine but vulnerable
  c. difficult to capture
  d. nonexistent   18. _____

19. In "Uphill," the real subject is which of the following?
  a. A typical traveler's journey
  b. A traveler who has a rough journey
  c. All of life, then death
  d. The challenges of life   19. _____

20. "The Erl-King" presents all of the following contests *except* one. Which one?
  a. Life and death
  b. Illusions and reality
  c. Protective love and destructive love
  d. Light and dark   20. _____

TEACHER'S NOTES

Unit 3: Poetry

UNIT ASSESSMENT STRATEGIES

UNIT TESTS The assessment tools provided with this program include **Mastery Tests, Analogy Tests,** and **Composition Tests**. These tests, covering materials in this section, are found on the pages that follow the **Teacher's Notes**. Answer Keys for these tests begin below.

ALTERNATE OR PORTFOLIO ASSESSMENT Since students vary widely in their aptitude and learning styles, this program provides evaluation tools for a broad range of assessment strategies. The forms and guidelines in this program provide rubrics for you to use in assessing compositions or for student or peer-group evaluation of compositions.

In addition to the unit tests described above, here is a list of other evaluation or assessment tools that are in the program:

- **Student Learning Options**—These suggested unit projects are listed on the unit interleaf pages in the *Annotated Teacher's Edition.*
- **Suggestions for Portfolio Assessment Projects**—This list of possible projects for student portfolios is located in the *Portfolio Assessment and Professional Support Materials* booklet.
- **Fine Arts and Instructional Transparencies**—These transparencies reinforce concepts covered in the unit. The transparencies are accompanied by Teacher's Notes and blackline masters with writing skills. The transparencies for each unit are located in the *Audiovisual Resource Binder.*
- **Evaluation Guides**—These forms are helpful for revising and assessing student papers, whether by you as instructor, by the student, or by peer evaluators. See the *Portfolio Assessment and Professional Support Materials* booklet.

For a variety of assessment and evaluation suggestions, see the *Portfolio Assessment and Professional Support Materials* booklet.

ANSWER KEYS

MASTERY TEST A

A.
1. b   6. c
2. a   7. d
3. b   8. b
4. d   9. a
5. b   10. a

B.
11. b   14. e
12. f   15. a
13. c   16. d

C. **For Composition**

Guidelines for Essay Topic

In a well-written essay on this topic, the student should:

1. Reflect an accurate understanding of the assignment
2. Identify the poem by stating the following information:
   - The name of the poem
   - The author of the poem
3. Paraphrase the poem. The following points should be included:
   - Restate all metaphors in literal language
   - Replace difficult words with simpler words
   - Make clear what is implied in the poem
4. Demonstrate effective use of the following writing skills:
   - Vocabulary

continued ☞

Teaching Resources D • *Adventures in Reading*   187

- Mechanics (spelling/punctuation/grammar)
- Sentence structure
- Organization (logical arrangement of ideas)

MASTERY TEST B

A.
1.	b	5.	d
2.	d	6.	a
3.	a	7.	c
4.	d	8.	b

B.
9.	b/e	12.	c/e
10.	a/e	13.	c
11.	a/e		

ANALOGY TEST

1. —E— lithe : stiff :: distinct : vague
   Lithe (limber) is an antonym of stiff just as distinct (clear) is an antonym of vague (unclear in thought or expression).

2. —A— scholar : books :: heathen : idols
   A scholar depends upon or uses books; a heathen (person who worships many gods and idols) depends upon or uses idols.

3. —C— sanctuary : holiness :: hospital : cleanliness
   A sanctuary (sacred place) is characterized by holiness just as a hospital is characterized by cleanliness.

4. —C— hungry : famished :: harmful : deadly
   Hungry differs in degree from famished (starving) in a similar way that harmful differs from deadly.

5. —B— fester : rot :: beguile : deceive
   Fester is a synonym of rot just as beguile is a synonym of deceive.

6. —C— armor : battle :: shroud : burial
   Armor is clothing used for battle; a shroud (burial cloth) is clothing used for burial.

7. —D— pavilion : tent :: satchel : valise
   A pavilion is a type of large, elegant tent. A satchel (a small suitcase or bag) is a type of valise (a piece of hand luggage).

8. —E— stupid : cunning :: generous : selfish
   Stupid is an antonym of cunning just as generous is an antonym of selfish.

9. —A— extravagance : bankruptcy :: laziness : failure
   Extravagance (wastefulness) can lead to or cause bankruptcy (a state of having no money) just as laziness can lead to or cause failure.

10. —B— frantic : frenetic :: ruddy : reddish
    Frantic is a synonym of frenetic (wild) just as ruddy is a synonym of reddish.

COMPOSITION TESTS

Student answers will vary, but students should write a composition response that has coherence and unity and that adequately covers the topic selected. Students should select a topic from among the choices given, express their opinions clearly in accordance with materials that they have read, and support their ideas with quotations or specific details from the selections. You may want to have students evaluate one another's compositions in cooperative groups. For assessment, you may wish to use one of the array of evaluation guides in the *Portfolio Assessment and Professional Support Materials* booklet.

NAME _____

CLASS _____ DATE _____ SCORE _____

Understanding Poetry

A. Recognizing Poetic Elements. Following are five excerpts from the poems in this unit. Read each excerpt carefully, and then answer the questions that follow. (*7 points each*)

> "I bring fresh showers for the thirsting flowers,
>   From the seas and the streams;
> I bear light shade for the leaves when laid
>   In their noonday dreams."

1. Which of the following *best* identifies the speaker in these lines?
   a. A professional gardener
   b. A cloud
   c. A fictional person
   d. The poet himself   1. _____

2. The diction of the lines can *best* be described as
   a. formal
   b. filled with dialect
   c. informal and jargon-filled
   d. abstract and remote   2. _____

> "'My father lived at Blenheim then,
>   Yon little stream hard by;
> They burnt his dwelling to the ground,
>   And he was forced to fly;
> So with his wife and child he fled,
> Nor had he where to rest his head.'"

3. The diction of these lines is all of the following *except*
   a. concrete   **c.** relatively informal
   b. onomatopoetic   **d.** conversational   3. _____

4. The speaker in this excerpt is which of the following?
   a. The poet himself
   b. An English soldier
   c. Some unidentified person
   d. A fictional character   4. _____

> "Not marble, nor the gilded monuments
> Of princes, shall outlive this powerful rime;
> But you shall shine more bright in these contents
> Than unswept stone, besmeared with sluttish time."

5. This is an excerpt taken from a
   a. literary ballad   **c.** witty nature poem
   b. sonnet   **d.** narrative poem   5. _____

continued ☞

> "I'll tell you how the sun rose—
> A ribbon at a time.
> The steeples swam in amethyst,
> The news like squirrels ran."

6. This excerpt can *best* be identified as
   a. part of a sonnet   **c.** a stanza from a lyric poem
   b. narrative poetry   **d.** an instance of formal diction   **6.** _____

7. The four lines contain all of the following *except*
   a. a simile   **c.** a speaker
   b. a metaphor   **d.** slangy diction   **7.** _____

> "Slowly, silently, now the moon
> Walks the night in her silver shoon; . . ."

8. In these two lines, we are given an example of
   a. blank verse   **c.** onomatopoeia
   b. personification   **d.** internal rhyme   **8.** _____

9. The words beginning with the letter *s* in these lines furnish an example of
   a. alliteration   **c.** parallelism
   b. onomatopoeia   **d.** repetition   **9.** _____

10. The lines are from a
   a. lyric poem   **c.** literary ballad
   b. narrative poem   **d.** dramatic poem   **10.** _____

B. **Understanding Poetic Techniques.** Match each lettered technique with its numbered definition. *(5 points each)*

   a. Folk ballad
   b. Simile
   c. Refrain
   d. Allusion
   e. Free verse
   f. Symbol

11. A comparison of two people or things, using *like* or *as*   **11.** _____

12. A specific image used to convey a wider meaning or idea   **12.** _____

13. A line, phrase, or group of lines repeated several times for a certain effect   **13.** _____

14. Poetry without a fixed metrical pattern or rhyme scheme   **14.** _____

15. A traditional poem telling a story, often with dialogue   **15.** _____

16. A reference to some historical event, literary work, or famous character   **16.** _____

C. **For Composition.** Select one of the poems in this unit. Read it carefully and then write a prose paraphrase of it. Avoid any temptation to quote phrases or sentences of the poem verbatim. Try to give your prose sentences variety. Try to make your paraphrase true to the sense of the poem—so that it makes the poem's content clear and perfectly understandable.

NAME _____

CLASS _____ DATE _____ SCORE _____

Applying Literature Skills

A. Understanding Poetry. Following are two poems. Read them carefully, and answer the questions that follow each. *(10 points each)*

The Pasture

I'm going out to clean the pasture spring;
I'll only stop to rake the leaves away
(And wait to watch the water clear, I may):
I shan't be gone long—You come too.

I'm going out to fetch the little calf
That's standing by the mother. It's so young
It totters when she licks it with her tongue.
I shan't be gone long—You come too.

—*Robert Frost*

1. The actions described in this poem help us to picture the speaker as a
   a. poet
   b. farmer
   c. teacher
   d. ranger
   1. _____

2. Two words that give exact, vivid pictures are
   a. *wait* and *watch* (line 3)
   b. *be* and *come* (line 4)
   c. *That's* and *It's* (line 6)
   d. *totters* and *licks* (line 7)
   2. _____

3. The poem contains examples of all of the following *except*
   a. a simile
   b. a refrain
   c. two specific "pictures"
   d. alliteration
   3. _____

All But Blind

All but blind
In his chambered hole
Gropes for worms
The four-clawed Mole.

All but blind   5
In the evening sky,
The hooded Bat
Twirls softly by.

All but blind
In the burning day   10
The Barn-Owl blunders
On her way.

And blind as are
These three to me,
So, blind to Someone   15
I must be.

—*Walter de la Mare*

continued ☞

4. In which stanza of this poem does the poet make a generalization?
  a. Stanza one   **c.** Stanza three
  b. Stanza two   **d.** Stanza four   **4.** _____

5. Three of the stanzas contain a picture-making verb that describes an action. Which stanza does not?
  a. Stanza one   **c.** Stanza three
  b. Stanza two   **d.** Stanza four   **5.** _____

6. The first stanza contains an example of
  a. inverted word order   **c.** personification
  b. a symbol   **d.** onomatopoeia   **6.** _____

7. Stanza three contains an example of which of the following?
  a. Simile   **c.** Alliteration
  b. Metaphor   **d.** Personification   **7.** _____

8. What most probably was the poet's reason for capitalizing the word *Someone* (line 15)?
  a. To indicate his puzzlement
  b. To indicate the Divinity
  c. To help make a witty image
  d. To indicate a reference to himself   **8.** _____

B. Recognizing Poetic Techniques.   Write the letter of the following poetic device or devices used in each quoted passage below. You may use an answer more than once. Some quotations use more than one device. (*4 points each*)
  a. Metaphor   **d.** Internal rhyme
  b. Simile   **e.** Personification
  c. Alliteration   **f.** Allusion

9. "Death is still working like a mole,
     And digs my grave at each remove"   **9.** _____

10. "I heard the trailing garments of the Night
      Sweep through her marble halls!"   **10.** _____

11. "But at my back I always hear
      Time's wingèd chariot hurrying near."   **11.** _____

12. "I will go back to the great sweet mother,
      Mother and lover of men, the sea."   **12.** _____

13. "In a summer season when soft was the sun"   **13.** _____

POETRY

Analogies. To solve the analogy problems that follow, use test
sentences to try all choices before deciding upon the correct answer.
Write the letter of your choice in the space provided.

QUESTION 1. _____
LITHE : STIFF ::
A. infant : baby
B. rest : sleep
C. pensive : thoughtful
D. garbage : trash
E. distinct : vague

QUESTION 2. _____
SCHOLAR : BOOKS ::
A. heathen : idols
B. wishes : desires
C. flesh : jowls
D. helpless : useless
E. lair : wolves

QUESTION 3. _____
SANCTUARY : HOLINESS ::
A. solitude : alone
B. instruction : elusive
C. hospital : cleanliness
D. formal : casualness
E. terrify : terror

QUESTION 4. _____
HUNGRY : FAMISHED ::
A. laugh : laughter
B. absurd : silly
C. harmful : deadly
D. vivid : dull
E. gather : collect

QUESTION 5. _____
FESTER : ROT ::
A. shout : whisper
B. beguile : deceive
C. embarrass : honor
D. inspire : discourage
E. nature : protection

QUESTION 6. _____
ARMOR : BATTLE ::
A. waft : air
B. tool : machine
C. shroud : burial
D. effort : endeavor
E. demon : devil

QUESTION 7. _____
PAVILION : TENT ::
A. home : garage
B. greenhouse : plant
C. eager : unwilling
D. satchel : valise
E. dwell : dwelling

QUESTION 8. _____
STUPID : CUNNING ::
A. brave : valiant
B. successful : clever
C. pleasant : cheerful
D. silly : giggling
E. generous : selfish

QUESTION 9. _____
EXTRAVAGANCE : BANKRUPTCY ::
A. laziness : failure
B. safety : expulsion
C. honest : honesty
D. applause : cheering
E. clothes : garments

QUESTION 10. _____
FRANTIC : FRENETIC ::
A. shine : shiny
B. ruddy : reddish
C. mechanic : repair
D. life : death
E. nondescript : specific

Composition
Test
A

Poetry
THE SPEAKER

The Face in the Mirror   *Robert Graves*   *(Page 298)*
from **The Cloud**   *Percy Bysshe Shelley*   *(Page 300)*

A. The speaker in a poem may be the poet or a character created by the poet. The speaker may even be a thing or an animal. Choose one of the poems listed above and give your impression of the speaker, using clues within the poem to describe the speaker's personality.

B. Select one of the poems listed above and show that the language of the poem is suited to its speaker.

_____

_____

_____

_____

_____

_____

_____

_____

_____

_____

_____

_____

_____

_____

_____

_____

_____

continued ☞

NAME _____

CLASS _____ DATE _____

_____

_____

_____

_____

_____

_____

_____

_____

_____

_____

_____

_____

_____

_____

_____

_____

_____

_____

Composition Test B

DICTION

To Satch	*Samuel Allen (Paul Vesey)*	*(Page 302)*
Cargoes	*John Masefield*	*(Page 304)*
Dream Deferred	*Langston Hughes*	*(Page 306)*

A. A poet depends on connotative meanings of words to arouse certain feelings or associations. Choose one of the poems listed above and discuss the poet's use of connotative meanings.

B. The diction in a poem may be formal or informal. Choose one example of each type and show how the diction of each poem is suited to its subject.

_____

_____

_____

_____

_____

_____

_____

_____

_____

_____

_____

_____

_____

_____

_____

continued ☞

_____

_____

_____

_____

_____

_____

_____

_____

_____

_____

_____

_____

_____

_____

_____

_____

_____

_____

_____

IMAGERY

A. Imagery in a poem may express a mood, tell a story, or convey an idea. Choose one of the poems listed above. Analyze the imagery and its function in the poem.

B. Imagery is often an effective means for creating contrast within a poem. Examine the use of imagery to create contrast in one of the poems listed above.

_____

_____

_____

_____

_____

_____

_____

_____

_____

_____

_____

_____

_____

_____

continued ☞

_____

_____

_____

_____

_____

_____

_____

_____

_____

_____

_____

_____

_____

_____

_____

_____

_____

_____

_____

| Composition Test **D** |

FIGURATIVE LANGUAGE

A. Figurative language is language that represents one thing in terms of another. In poetry, figurative language expresses original and imaginative relationships between things. Figurative language includes such figures of speech as *similes, metaphors, personifications,* and *symbols.* Select one example of each of these figures of speech in the poems listed above and explain its function in the poem.

B. Explain the difference between *simile* and *metaphor*, using any *four* poems listed above.

C. Analyze the poet's use of figurative language in one of these poems: "The Day Is Done," "I'll Tell You How the Sun Rose," "Silver," or "A Song of the Moon."

_____

_____

_____

_____

_____

_____

_____

_____

_____

_____

_____

continued ☞

_____

_____

_____

_____

_____

_____

_____

_____

_____

_____

_____

_____

_____

_____

_____

_____

_____

_____

_____

Composition Test E

SOUND PATTERNS

A. *Rhyme, rhythm, alliteration, assonance,* and *parallelism* are all devices of repetition. Define each term and give at least two examples of each one from the poems listed above.

B. Describe the rhythm and rhyme scheme of any one of these poems: "The Destruction of Sennacherib," "Eldorado," or "The Shell."

C. A poem may have a regular rhythm or an irregular rhythm. Choose one poem of each type from the list above and show how the rhythmic pattern is suitable to the subject of the poem.

_____

_____

_____

_____

_____

_____

_____

_____

_____

_____

_____

_____

continued ☞

NAME _____

CLASS _____ DATE _____

_____

_____

_____

_____

_____

_____

_____

_____

_____

_____

_____

_____

_____

_____

_____

_____

_____

_____

_____

_____

_____

_____

Composition Test F

For information regarding permissioned material included on this page, see pages ii–iv.

STRUCTURES

A. In order to work, a poem has to be organized into a structure that is appropriate to its content. One important unit in poems is the *stanza*. Describe the stanza pattern (line length, number of lines, rhyme scheme, and rhythm) of "Sonnet 55."

B. Compare and contrast the Petrarchan sonnet and the Shakespearean sonnet, using "The Sound of the Sea" and "Sonnet 55" to illustrate similarities and differences in structure.

C. *Free verse,* as you have learned, does not have a fixed rhythm, rhyme scheme, or line length. Yet, in order to succeed, a poem must have a structure. Describe the structure Shapiro devises in "Manhole Covers."

D. How do the poets use line arrangements to match content in "400-meter Freestyle" and "The Time We Climbed Snake Mountain"?

_____

_____

_____

_____

_____

_____

_____

_____

_____

_____

continued ☞

_____

_____

_____

_____

_____

_____

_____

_____

_____

_____

_____

_____

_____

_____

_____

_____

_____

_____

_____

NAME _____

CLASS _____ DATE _____ SCORE _____

TONE

A. The *tone* of a poem shows the poet's or the speaker's attitude toward the subject. The tone of a poem can be colored by diction, imagery, rhythm, sound, and other elements. Choose one of the poems listed above and describe its overall tone. Cite evidence from the poem to support your conclusion.

B. Although a poem generally has an overall tone, there may be shifts of mood within a work. Choose one of the poems listed above and analyze its shifts or changes in tone.

_____

_____

_____

_____

_____

_____

_____

_____

_____

_____

_____

_____

_____

_____

continued ☞

_____

_____

_____

_____

_____

_____

_____

_____

_____

_____

_____

_____

_____

_____

_____

_____

_____

_____

_____

_____

NAME _____

CLASS _____ DATE _____ SCORE _____

LYRIC POETRY

A. A lyric poem is rich in musical devices. Analyze the verbal music in one of the poems listed above.

B. A lyric poem is generally a short poem that expresses the speaker's emotion. Choose one of the poems listed above and discuss its speaker's response to a person, place, object, or idea.

continued ☞

_____

_____

_____

_____

_____

_____

_____

_____

_____

_____

_____

_____

_____

_____

_____

_____

_____

_____

_____

Composition Test

I

NARRATIVE POETRY

Lord Randal	*Anonymous*	*(Page 384)*
All in green went my love riding	*E. E. Cummings*	*(Page 386)*
The Castle	*Edwin Muir*	*(Page 389)*

A. Discuss the characteristics of the *ballad*, citing examples from "Lord Randal" and "All in green went my love riding."

B. How does the speaker in "The Castle" give his story universal relevance?

_____

_____

_____

_____

_____

_____

_____

_____

_____

_____

_____

_____

_____

_____

_____

_____

_____

_____

continued ☞

_____

_____

_____

_____

_____

_____

_____

_____

_____

_____

_____

_____

_____

_____

_____

_____

_____

_____

_____

_____

_____

Composition
Test
J

For information regarding permissioned material included on this page, see pages ii–iv.

DRAMATIC POETRY

The Seven Ages of Man	*William Shakespeare*	*(Page 391)*
Uphill	*Christina Rossetti*	*(Page 394)*
The Erl-King	*Johann Wolfgang von Goethe*	*(Page 395)*

A. Dramatic poems present characters who speak to other characters or to an audience. What does Jaques reveal about himself in "The Seven Ages of Man"?

B. "Uphill" is in the form of a dialogue between two voices. Tell who the speakers are and explain the different levels of meaning in the poem.

C. "The Erl-King" has three speakers. Tell who they are and explain how their dialogue establishes atmosphere and reveals theme.

_____

_____

_____

_____

_____

_____

_____

_____

_____

_____

_____

_____

HRW material copyrighted under notice appearing earlier in this work.

continued ☞